ECONOMICS 3D0

TABLE OF CONTENTS & ACKNOWLEDGEMENTS

	PAGE

The Labour Market in Canada and the United States
Since the Last Recession
    Bernard, A. and Usalcas, J.
    <u>Economic Insights</u>, 036
    © 2014 Statistics Canada
    Reprinted with permission.
        1

Full-time Employment, 1976 to 2014
    Hou, F. et al
    <u>Economic Insights</u>, 049
    © 2015 Statistics Canada
    Reprinted with permission.
        9

A Shred of Credible Evidence on the Long-Run Elasticity of
Labour Supply
    Ashenfelter, O. Doran, K. and Schaller, B.
    <u>Economica</u>, 77. 308
    © 2010 London School of Economics
    Reprinted with permission.
        19

The Ups and Downs of Minimum Wage
    Galarneau, D. and Fecteau, E.
    <u>Insights on Canadian Society</u>, Catalogue no. 75-006-X
    © 2014 Statistics Canada
    Reprinted with permission.
        33

The Cumulative Earnings of Postsecondary Graduates Over 20 Years:
Results by Field of Study
    Yuri, O. and Frenette, M.
    <u>Economic Insights</u>
    © 2014 Statistics Canada
    Reprinted with permission.
        45

Unemployment Dynamics Among Canada's Youth
    Bernard, A.
    <u>Economic Insights</u>, 24
    © 2013 Statistics Canada
    Reprinted with permission.
        53

The Labour Market in Canada and the United States since the Last Recession

by André Bernard, Analytical Studies Branch and Jeannine Usalcas, Labour Statistics Division

This *Economic Insights* article reports on recent labour market trends in both Canada and the United States since the last recession. The data for Canada come from Statistics Canada's Labour Force Survey (LFS), while those for the United States come from the Current Population Survey (CPS), a survey produced for the Bureau of Labor Statistics. For the purposes of comparison, the Canadian data have been adjusted to follow the concepts used in the United States. Unless indicated otherwise, the data for both countries are monthly and are seasonally adjusted.

Given the integrated nature of the U.S. and Canadian economies, cyclical fluctuations in the United States tend to have an impact on economic activity in Canada. Comparisons between the Canadian and U.S. labour markets, therefore, generate a high level of interest.[1] In fact, although the impact of U.S. economic downturns on the Canadian economy has varied greatly from case to case, previous recessions in both countries have often been synchronized (Cross 2009).

In the United States, the recession that started in December 2007[2] had a profound impact on the U.S. labour market, and has been described as the most severe recession of the post-war period (Elsby, Hobijn and Sahin 2010). In Canada, the 2008–2009 recession also resulted in considerable job losses, but has been less severe than recessions that started in 1981 and in 1990 (Cross 2011). After the recession, employment growth in both countries followed an upward trend. However, the rate of growth was not steady, and average monthly employment growth in both countries was slower in 2013 than in 2012.

In Canada, information on the current state of the labour market is collected through Statistics Canada's Labour Force Survey (LFS). In the United States, household labour market information is taken from the Current Population Survey (CPS), a survey conducted for the Bureau of Labor Statistics.[3] Both are monthly surveys that use largely similar methodologies. The LFS sample is approximately 56,000 households, while the sample for the CPS is approximately 60,000 households.

There are, nonetheless, some conceptual differences between the two surveys. Therefore, adjustments are made to the Canadian data to make them coherent with the U.S. concepts, so that the data from the two countries can be compared (Sunter 1998; Usalcas and Bowlby 2002; Ferrao 2009; Zmitrowicz and Khan, 2014). These adjustments are presented in the appendix.

Adjustments made to the data can affect their interpretation. For example, if the unemployment rates of the two countries were to be compared without taking these adjustments into account, the U.S. unemployment rate would have fallen below the Canadian rate in December 2013, after being higher the previous five years. In reality, Canada's unemployment rate in that month, adjusted for the purposes of comparison with the U.S. rate, was still 0.6 percentage points lower than the U.S. rate.

In this article, a set of indicators for the pre-recession period up to June 2014 is compared, to obtain a comparative profile of the state of the labour market in both countries. The indicators presented are employment, the employment rate, the unemployment rate, and the participation rate. **All of the Canadian data have been adjusted to the U.S. concepts, to allow for direct comparisons.**

Decline in employment more severe in the United States than in Canada during the last recession

Although the last recession led to significant employment losses in both countries, employment losses in the United States were larger - even after accounting for the differences in the size of the two economies - and extended over a longer period of time than losses in Canada.

---

1. See, for example, Zmitrowicz and Khan, 2014, Karabegovic et al. 2012.
2. For the start and end dates of U.S. recessions, see the National Bureau of Economic Research (NBER): www.nber.org/cycles.html. (accessed July 22, 2014).
3. The Current Employment Statistics (CES) program is a survey of approximately 144,000 businesses and government agencies in the United States. It is closer in concepts to the Survey of Employment, Payrolls and Hours (SEPH) in Canada. In this article, data from the U.S. Current Population Survey are used in order to ensure consistency with Canada's Labour Force Survey.

In Canada, employment adjusted to U.S. concepts contracted by 400,000 jobs from peak (October 2008) to trough (July 2009)—a 2.3% decline over nine months.[4] By comparison, employment in the United States contracted by 8.6 million from peak (November 2007) to trough (December 2009)—a 5.9% decrease over a 25-month period (Chart 1).

Chart 1
Employment growth in Canada and the United States, seasonally adjusted, January 2007 to June 2014

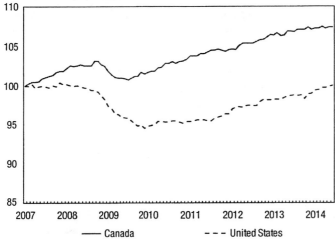

Note: The Canadian data have been adjusted to make them comparable with the U.S. data.
Sources: Statistics Canada, Labour Force Survey; and U.S. Bureau of Labor Statistics, Current Population Survey.

Employment growth in both countries slowed in 2013, but increased in the United States in early 2014

In Canada, the decline of 400,000 in employment during the downturn was regained in the 16 months from July 2009 to November 2010. Employment then continued an upward trend, increasing on average by 15,900 workers each month until June 2014—an average monthly increase of 0.1%. However, the pace of employment growth has not been steady. Average monthly employment growth was 26,000 in 2012, before slowing to 8,900 in 2013, and to 7,100 in the first six months of 2014.

In the United States, employment expanded on average by 152,000 per month from the low in December 2009 until June 2014, a pace that was proportionally similar to that of Canada. In June 2014, the number of employed individuals in the United States was, therefore, close to, but still below the peak it reached in November 2007.

As in Canada, growth in the United States accelerated in 2012, before slowing in 2013. Employment increased by an average of 115,000 during each month of 2013 in the United States, as compared with 198,000 during 2012. However, employment growth strengthened during the first six months of 2014, at an average increase of 273,000 each month.

Employment growth similar to working-age population growth in both countries

The employment rate corresponds to the percentage of the working-age population that is employed. It allows the interpretation of employment growth in relation to population growth. Employment growth that is greater than population growth can be indicative of an improvement in the state of the labour market. The employment rate increases (decreases) when employment growth is higher (lower) than working-age population growth.

In Canada, the employment rate, adjusted to U.S. concepts, declined during the 2008–2009 recession, falling from a historic high of 64.4%, in February 2008, to a cyclical low of 62.0% in July 2009 (Chart 2). The July 2009 employment rate was the lowest since March 2002.

Chart 2
Employment rates in Canada and the United States, seasonally adjusted, January 2007 to June 2014

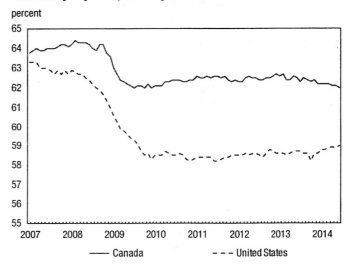

Note: The Canadian data have been adjusted to make them comparable with the U.S. data.
Sources: Statistics Canada, Labour Force Survey; and U.S. Bureau of Labor Statistics, Current Population Survey.

Since then, the rate has changed little, and stood at 62.0% in June 2014. The stability of Canada's employment rate since 2009 indicates that the rate of employment growth has not surpassed working-age population growth.

In the United States, the employment rate decreased from a cyclical high of 63.3%, in March 2007, to a low of 58.2%, in November 2010, the lowest employment rate observed since 1983. This decline in the employment rate was more significant than in the previous three recessions, and was more than double the corresponding decline in Canada. Subsequently, the employment rate in the United States did not change much.

---

4. See Larochelle-Côté and Gilmore (2009) for a detailed account of Canada's employment downturn during this period.

As in Canada, employment growth in the United States since 2010 was, therefore, similar to the growth of the working-age population.

It is not unprecedented for Canada to have a declining employment rate during a recession, followed by stability at relatively low levels. During the 1990–1992 recession, the employment rate in Canada declined sharply, and remained relatively low for much of the 1990s, before beginning to trend upward (Chart 3). It was not until the end of 2002 that the employment rate returned to its pre-recession level. For this reason, the employment rate was lower in Canada than in the United States, throughout the 1990s until the end of 2002.

Chart 3
Employment rates in Canada and the United States, annual, 1976 to 2013

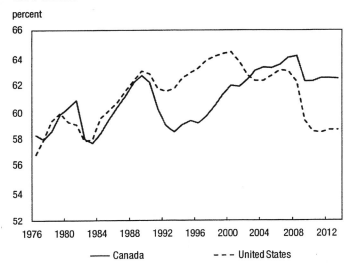

Note: The Canadian data have been adjusted to make them comparable with the U.S. data.
Sources: Statistics Canada, Labour Force Survey; and U.S. Bureau of Labor Statistics, Current Population Survey.

The employment rate in the United States trended downward over the 2000 to 2004 period and during the last recession[5], while, in Canada, it continued to trend upward until the start of the last downturn. Because of these diverging trends, the employment rate in Canada has remained above the rate in the United States since November 2002.

The most significant declines in the employment rate in both countries since the recession were recorded among youth

In both countries, declines in employment rates since the last recession were more significant for youth than for any other age group (Chart 4). In Canada, from the pre-recession peak of February 2008 until June 2014, the employment rate among youth, aged 16 to 24, fell by 5.0 percentage points to 58.7%. Over the same period, the employment rate among adults, aged 25 to 54, declined 2.0 percentage points to 80.6%.

Chart 4
Employment rates change from pre-recession peak to June 2014, in Canada and the United States, seasonally adjusted, 2007 to 2014

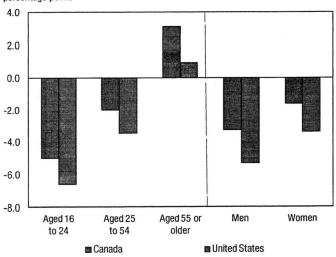

Note: Changes for both countries represent the percentage point differences between their respective pre-recession peaks for the overall employment rate in both countries, which correspond to March 2007 in the United States and February 2008 in Canada, to the most recent month of available data, June 2014. The Canadian data have been adjusted to make them comparable with the U.S. data.
Sources: Statistics Canada, Labour Force Survey; and U.S. Bureau of Labor Statistics, Current Population Survey.

In the United States, from its pre-recession peak of March 2007 to June 2014, the youth employment rate fell 6.6 percentage points to 47.5%, while it declined 3.5 percentage points to 76.7%, among individuals aged 25 to 54.

In both countries, the decline in the employment rate in recent years has been more significant for men than for women.

The employment rate for Americans aged 55 and over did not trend downward during or after the recession, while the rate for their Canadian counterparts rose, reaching a record high in June 2014. This finding is consistent with recent trends suggesting the postponement of retirement among older workers (Galarneau and Carrière, 2012).

---

5. See Moffitt, 2012, for an analysis of the factors that contributed to the decline of the employment rate in the United States during that period.

The unemployment rate more than doubled in the United States during the last recession

Since employment losses were greater in the United States than in Canada, the increase in the unemployment rate during the recession was more substantial in the United States (Chart 5). The increases in both countries were significant for all age groups (Charts 6 and 7).

Chart 5
Unemployment rates in Canada and the United States, seasonally adjusted, January 2007 to June 2014

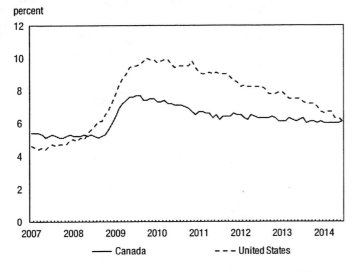

Note: The Canadian data have been adjusted to make them comparable with the U.S. data.
Sources: Statistics Canada, Labour Force Survey; and U.S. Bureau of Labor Statistics, Current Population Survey.

In August 2008, Canada's unemployment rate, adjusted to U.S. concepts, was at its lowest level since 1976, at 5.1%. In the wake of the recession, the unemployment rate rose by 2.6 percentage points to 7.7%, in July 2009. It then decreased gradually over the following four years. In the United States, the unemployment rate more than doubled during the downturn, from 4.4% in May 2007 to 10.0% in October 2009, before beginning to decline.

Chart 6
Unemployment rates in Canada by age groups, seasonally adjusted, January 2007 to June 2014

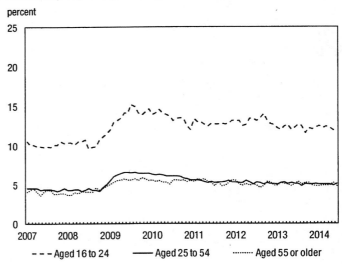

Note: The Canadian data have been adjusted to make them comparable with the U.S. data.
Sources: Statistics Canada, Labour Force Survey; and U.S. Bureau of Labor Statistics, Current Population Survey.

Chart 7
Unemployment rates in the United States by age groups, seasonally adjusted, January 2007 to June 2014

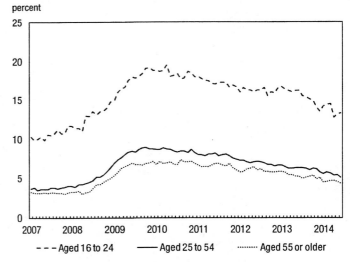

Note: The Canadian data have been adjusted to make them comparable with the U.S. data.
Sources: Statistics Canada, Labour Force Survey; and U.S. Bureau of Labor Statistics, Current Population Survey.

Unemployment rate higher in the United States than in Canada since 2008, but the gap has closed

The unemployment rate in the United States was higher than in Canada from May 2008 to May 2014. This contrasted with historic patterns where the U.S. unemployment rate remained consistently lower than that of Canada since the early 1980s (Chart 8).

In November 2010, the difference between the unemployment rates in the United States and in Canada was 3.1 percentage points—the largest difference in Canada's favour recorded since 1976. The gap between the two unemployment rates then gradually narrowed, as the decline in the unemployment rate in the United States was more rapid than the decline in Canada. In June 2014, the two unemployment rates were identical, at 6.1% (Chart 5).

Chart 8
Unemployment rates in Canada and the United States, annual, 1976 to 2013

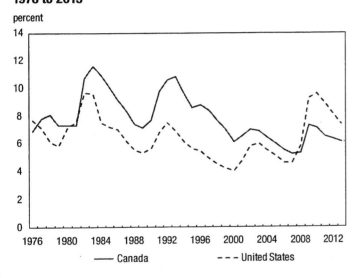

Note: The Canadian data have been adjusted to make them comparable with the U.S. data.
Sources: Statistics Canada, Labour Force Survey; and U.S. Bureau of Labor Statistics, Current Population Survey.

The decline in labour force participation has been driving the decline in the unemployment rate in recent years, in both countries

As employment growth did not outpace working-age population growth, declining unemployment rates in Canada and the United States, over the past four years, have been largely driven by declines in labour force participation. The participation rate—the percentage of the working-age population that is employed or looking for work—has declined, in both countries, since the beginning of the last downturn. The decrease in the participation rate has been more pronounced in the United States than in Canada, which helps explain the larger decrease in the unemployment rate in the United States as compared with Canada in recent years (Chart 9).

Chart 9
Labour force participation rates in Canada and the United States, seasonally adjusted, January 2007 to June 2014

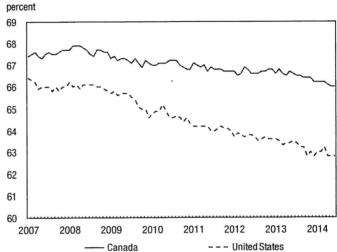

Note: The Canadian data have been adjusted to make them comparable with the U.S. data.
Sources: Statistics Canada, Labour Force Survey; and U.S. Bureau of Labor Statistics, Current Population Survey.

In Canada, the participation rate adjusted to U.S. concepts was at its pre-recession peak in April 2008, at 67.9%. The rate has since declined to 66.0% as of May and June 2014. This was the lowest participation rate in Canada since August 2001.

In the United States, the participation rate was 66.4% in January 2007, before declining 3.6 percentage points to June 2014. The U.S. participation rate stood at 62.8% in June 2014, for the fifth time in the past nine months, the lowest level since March 1978.

Since 2002, labour force participation has been higher in Canada than in the United States (Chart 10). In recent years, the larger decrease in the U.S participation rate has widened the gap between the rates in the two countries, which was 3.2 points in favour of Canada in June 2014 (Chart 9).

Chart 10
Labour force participation rates in Canada and the United States, annual, 1976 to 2013

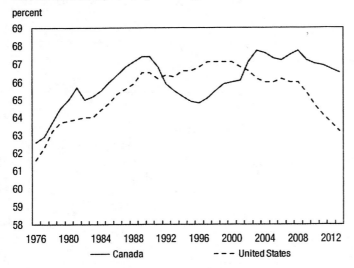

Note: The Canadian data have been adjusted to make them comparable with the U.S. data.
Sources: Statistics Canada, Labour Force Survey; and U.S. Bureau of Labor Statistics, Current Population Survey.

Chart 11
Labour force participation rates in Canada and the United States, 25 to 54 years old, seasonally adjusted, January 2007 to June 2014

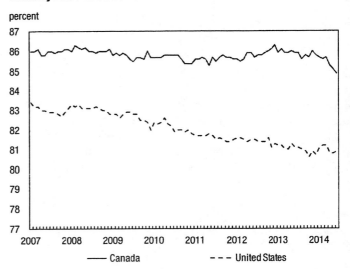

Note: The Canadian data have been adjusted to make them comparable with the U.S. data.
Sources: Statistics Canada, Labour Force Survey; and U.S. Bureau of Labor Statistics, Current Population Survey.

Labour force participation down among prime-age workers in the United States

Because the share of older workers in the working-age population has increased over time and older workers tend to have lower participation rates, an aging population in both countries can put significant downward pressure on the overall labour force participation rate (Janzen, 2014, Zmitrowicz and Khan, 2014). Trends in labour force participation rates among prime-aged workers are informative in that they are less likely to be affected by population aging (Zmitrowicz and Khan, 2014).

In Canada, the participation rate among prime-age workers, aged 25 to 54, remained relatively stable during and after the recession, before declining 1.1 percentage points to 84.9% from November 2013 to June 2014. In the United States, the decline in the participation rate was larger and more gradual. At 80.9% in June 2014, it was 2.5 percentage points lower than it was in January 2007 (Chart 11).

In both countries, labour force participation was down among youth and up among older workers

In Canada, as in the United States, the labour force participation of youth has declined significantly, while that of older workers has in fact increased (Chart 12).

In Canada, from the pre-recession peak of April 2008 until June 2014, the participation rate among youth, aged 16 to 24, fell by 4.6 percentage points to 66.8%. Conversely, the participation rate for those aged 55 and over increased over the same period, from 34.0% to 37.5%.

A similar phenomenon has been observed in the United States. From the pre-recession high of January 2007 until June 2014, the participation rate among Americans aged 16 to 24 fell from 60.7% to 54.7%. During that time, workers aged 55 and over recorded an increase in their participation rate, from 38.0% to 40.0%.

Chart 12
Labour force participation rate changes from pre-recession peak to June 2014, in Canada and the United States, seasonally adjusted, 2007 to 2014

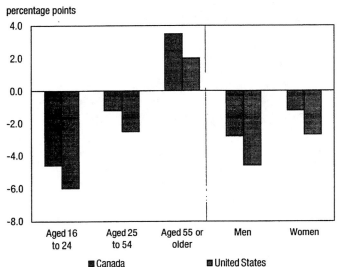

Note: Changes for both countries represent the percentage point differences between their respective pre-recession peaks for the overall labour force participation rate in both countries, which correspond to January 2007 in the United States and April 2008 in Canada, to the most recent month of available data, June 2014. The Canadian data have been adjusted to make them comparable with the U.S. data.
Sources: Statistics Canada, Labour Force Survey; and U.S. Bureau of Labor Statistics, Current Population Survey.

In Canada, as in the United States, men contributed more than women to the decline in the overall participation rate since the last recession. In Canada, from April 2008 until June 2014, the participation rate among men fell 2.8 percentage points to 70.5%, while it declined 1.2 percentage points to 61.5% among women. In the United States, from January 2007 to June 2014, men's participation rate fell 4.6 percentage points to 69.2% while women's participation rate declined by 2.7 percentage points to 56.8%.

Summary

This article has presented a set of indicators on the state of the labour market in Canada and in the United States, from the pre-recession period up to June 2014. The Canadian data has been adjusted to make them directly comparable with U.S. data. Through comparative analysis, a number of similarities and differences between the two countries have been identified.

The last recession resulted in more severe employment losses in the United States than in Canada. Proportionally, employment losses in the United States were more than double those in Canada, and lasted longer.

Since then, employment in both countries has increased at approximately the same rate, and has not exceeded the rate of growth of the working-age population. Accordingly, the employment rate remains below the pre-recession level in both countries. Since the beginning of 2014, however, employment growth has been higher in the United States than in Canada.

Since the end of the recession, the unemployment rate in both countries has declined, but the decreases have been largely driven by decreases in labour force participation. The decline in the participation rate in the United States has been more pronounced than in Canada, notably among prime-age workers. Therefore, the decrease in the unemployment rate has been more pronounced in the United States. Although Canada's unemployment rate had been lower than that of the United States since May 2008, the gap between the rates has now closed.

Appendix: adjustments to Canadian data

This section details the adjustments that must be made to the Canadian data from the Labour Force Survey (LFS) to make them directly comparable with the U.S. data from the Current Population Survey (CPS).

First, those aged 15 must be removed from the LFS, as they are not surveyed in the CPS. This change affects both the employed and unemployed populations.

The other changes affect only the unemployed population. Three groups of people, considered unemployed in Canada, are deemed to not be participating in the labour force in the United States: (1) people who were looking for work, but who looked only at job ads; (2) people who had not looked for work, but who reported that they had a job that would start in the next four weeks; and (3) people who had reported that they were not available to work because of personal or family responsibilities. These three groups of people were, therefore, removed from the unemployed population in the LFS, and were added to the population of people not participating in the labour force.

Conversely, full-time students who report that they are looking for full-time work are not considered participants in the labour force in Canada, but are considered to be part of the unemployed population in the United States. These people were, therefore, removed from the population that was not participating in the labour force in the LFS, and were added to the unemployed population.

When these adjustments are made, the unemployment rate is generally lower than the headline rate published by Statistics Canada (Chart 13), while the employment rate is generally higher than official estimates. The magnitude of these differences can vary over long periods of time. On average from 2007 to 2013, the difference between the adjusted and unadjusted unemployment rates was 0.9 percentage points while the difference between the adjusted and unadjusted employment rate was 0.7 percentage points. In recent years, there has generally been little difference between the adjusted and unadjusted Canadian participation rates.

Chart 13
Unemployment rates in Canada (official and adjusted to U.S. concepts) and the United States, annual, 1976 to 2013

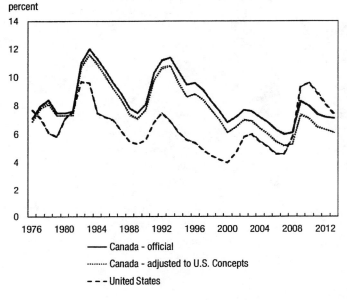

Note: The Canadian data have been adjusted to make them comparable with the U.S. data.
Sources: Statistics Canada, Labour Force Survey; and U.S. Bureau of Labor Statistics, Current Population Survey.

References

Cross, Philip. 2009. "The impact of recessions in the United States on Canada." *Canadian Economic Observer*. Catalogue no. 11-010. Statistics Canada. March.

Cross, Philip. 2011. "How did the 2008-2010 recession and recovery compare with previous cycles?" *Canadian Economic Observer*. Catalogue no. 11-010. Statistics Canada. January.

Elsby, Michael W, Bart Hobijn and Aysegul Sahin, 2010. The Labor Market in the Great Recession. NBER Working Paper 15979, National Bureau of Economic Research, Cambridge. May.

Ferrao, Vincent. 2009. "The recent labour market situation in Canada and the United States." *Perspectives on Labour and Income*, Catalogue no. 75-001. Statistics Canada. March.

Galarneau, Diane and Yves Carrière. 2012. "How many years to retirement?" *Insights on Canadian Society*. Catalogue no. 75-006. Statistics Canada. December.

Janzen, Nathan. 2014. "What explains the decline in Canada's labour force participation rate?" RBC Economics Research, May.

Karabegovic, Amela, Nachum Gabler and Niels Veldhuis. 2012. *Measuring Labour Markets in Canada and the United States*. 2012 Edition. Fraser Institute. September.

LaRochelle-Côté, Sébastien and Jason Gilmore, 2009. "Canada's Employment Downturn." *Perspectives on Labour and Income*, Catalogue No. 75-001. Statistics Canada. December.

Moffitt, Robert A. 2012. The U.S. Employment-Population Reversal in the 2000s: Facts and Explanations. National Bureau of Economic Research, Working Paper no. 18520. November.

Sunter, Deborah. 1998. "Canada - US Labour Market Comparison" *Canadian Economic Observer*, Catalogue No. 11-010. Statistics Canada. December.

Usalcas, Jeannine and Geoff Bowlby, 2002. "The Labour Market: Up North, Down South" *Perspectives on Labour and Income*, Catalogue No. 75-001 Statistics Canada. December.

Zmitrowicz, Konrad and Mikael Khan. 2014. "*Beyond the Unemployment Rate: Assessing Canadian and U.S. Labour Markets Since the Great Recession*" *Bank of Canada Review*. Spring.

Full-time Employment, 1976 to 2014

by René Morissette, Feng Hou, and Grant Schellenberg, Social Analysis and Modelling Division

This *Economic Insights* article addresses three questions: (1) How has the full-time employment rate—the percentage of the population employed full time—evolved since the mid-1970s overall? (2) How has the full-time employment rate changed across age groups, education levels, sex, and regions? (3) To what extent have movements in full-time employment rates been driven by changes in the socio-demographic characteristics of Canadians and by changes in labour market participation rates, unemployment rates, and part-time employment rates? The study combines data from the Labour Force Survey, the Census of Population, the Survey of Work History of 1981, and the National Household Survey of 2011 to examine these issues. Attention is restricted to individuals who are aged 17 to 64 and who are not full-time students.[1]

Introduction

Full-time employment is an important labour market indicator from the perspective of both labour supply and demand. On the supply side, full-time jobs are the main channel through which working-age Canadians generate income and are a key determinant of financial well-being. Full-time employment also reveals information about the success of some groups in the labour market. For groups who have a strong attachment to the labour market, the proportion employed full time, along with the unemployment rate, is an important dimension along which success can be gauged. On the demand side, the creation of full-time jobs is one indicator of economic performance, with commentators often drawing attention to the share of employment growth accounted for by full-time jobs.

The full-time employment rate is defined as the share of the total population aged 17 to 64 employed at least 30 hours per week in their main job (i.e., the job involving the greatest numbers of weekly hours).[2] It may have changed over the last few

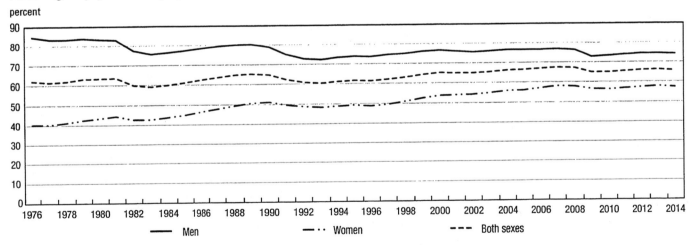

Chart 1
Percentage of population employed full time in their main job, by sex, 1976 to 2014

— Men   — ·· Women   - - - Both sexes

Note: The population consists of individuals aged 17 to 64 who are not full-time students. Full-time employment is defined as working usually 30 hours or more per week. The main job is the job with the greatest number of weekly work hours.
Source: Statistics Canada, Labour Force Survey, 1976 to 2014.

1. Full-time students are excluded because the vast majority of them are not available for full-time work and thus, are quite unlikely to be employed full time. Individuals aged less than 17 are excluded because compulsory schooling laws in many provinces require them to attend school full time.
2. Trends in full-time employment rates are shown using a full-time employment concept based on usual hours worked in the main job. The definition of usual hours changed with the re-design of the Labour Force Survey (LFS) in 1997. As the *Guide to the Labour Force Survey* (p. 18) states: "Prior to January 1997, usual hours were the number of hours usually worked by the respondent in a typical week, regardless of whether they were paid. Beginning January 1997, usual hours for employees refer to their normal paid or contract hours, not counting any overtime." To ensure that the findings of the study are not affected by this definitional change, full-time employment rates based on actual hours worked during the reference week were also computed (excluding from the computation of these alternative rates individuals who were employed but absent from work during the reference week). All of the conclusions obtained regarding trends in full-time employment rates hold under these alternative full-time employment rates.

decades for various reasons. For example, employers' propensity to offer full-time jobs may have increased or decreased in response to changing economic conditions and the competitive environments in which they operate. Evolving preferences and attitudes, such as the desire to balance work and family, may have increased preferences for part-time employment, while evolving transitions over the life course, such as school-to-work transitions or retirement, may have affected full-time employment rates within age groups.

The trends

In aggregate, the percentage of people employed full time has increased slightly since the mid-1970s. Of all individuals aged 17 to 64 who were not attending school full time, 66% were employed full time as employees or self-employed workers in 2014, up from 62% in 1976 (Table 1).[3] The full-time employment rate reached a high of 68% in 2007, prior to the last recession, following a secular increase in the percentage of women holding full-time jobs (Chart 1).

Indeed, the overall increase observed since the mid-1970s masks divergent trends among men and women. The proportion of men working full time fell by 10 percentage points from 1976 to 2014. Virtually all this decline occurred between the mid-1970s and the early 1990s, with the rate remaining around 75% since then (Chart 1). In contrast, the full-time employment rate of women increased by 17 percentage points over the 1976-to-2014 period, rising from 40% to 57%.

These aggregate trends also conceal important differences across age groups. In particular, large declines in full-time employment have been observed among youth (again excluding full-time students). From 1976 to 2014, the full-time employment rate declined by about 18 percentage points among men aged 17 to 24 and by about 11 percentage points among women in that age group (Table 2).[4] A substantial portion of these declines occurred between 2007 and 2014 (Chart 2). A similar pattern was evident among men aged 25 to 29, with the full-time employment rate declining by 10 percentage points from 1976 to 2014. About two-fifths of that decline occurred between 2007 and 2014. The full-time employment rate of women aged 25 to 29 also declined in recent years, offsetting some of the gains observed earlier.[5]

In addition to declines among youth, the full-time employment rate fell among men in their 'prime' working years, with an 8-percentage-point drop observed among men aged 30 to 54. As was the case for younger men, the rate fell substantially between the mid-1970s and the early 1990s (Chart 3).

An even larger decline was observed among men aged 55 to 64, at least until the mid-1990s.[6] Among women aged 25 or older, substantial increases in the full-time employment rate were observed.

Quite clearly, the shares of youth and of men engaged in full-time employment fell since the mid-1970s. While one might view the declines among younger and older male workers as consequences of changing life course or retirement transitions, it is not obvious what might account for the decline among men aged 30 to 54 (Chart 3).

Table 1

Percentage of population employed full time in their main job, by sex, 1976 to 2014

	Percentage of population aged 17 to 64 employed full time as		Percentage of population aged 25 to 54 employed full time as	
	Employees	Employees or self-employed	Employees	Employees or self-employed
	percent			
Both sexes				
1976	55.1	62.1	55.7	64.0
1981	56.3	63.6	57.7	66.6
1989	56.8	65.4	60.6	70.4
1992	52.3	61.0	57.0	66.8
1995	52.6	61.7	57.7	67.9
1997	52.2	62.1	57.2	68.3
2007	57.6	67.6	63.3	74.3
2014	56.8	65.8	63.4	73.1
Men				
1976	72.8	84.4	76.2	89.8
1981	71.0	82.9	74.2	88.5
1989	67.1	80.2	71.4	86.2
1992	59.9	73.0	65.2	79.8
1995	60.6	74.0	66.1	80.9
1997	60.1	74.6	65.3	81.3
2007	62.8	76.9	68.4	83.8
2014	61.6	74.2	68.4	82.0
Women				
1976	37.7	40.2	35.2	38.0
1981	41.7	44.4	41.0	44.5
1989	46.6	50.6	49.7	54.6
1992	44.7	49.0	48.9	53.8
1995	44.7	49.5	49.4	54.9
1997	44.2	49.6	49.2	55.4
2007	52.4	58.2	58.2	64.7
2014	52.0	57.4	58.4	64.2

Note: The population consists of individuals aged 17 to 64 who are not full-time students. Full-time employment is defined as working usually 30 hours or more per week. The main job is the job with the greatest number of weekly work hours.
Source: Statistics Canada, Labour Force Survey, 1976 to 2014.

---

3. The percentage of individuals holding full-time jobs as employees increased from 55% to 57%.
4. Youth unemployment rates were fairly similar in 1976 and 2014. Of all men aged 17 to 24 who were not full-time students, 14.3% were unemployed in 2014, compared with 13.5 % in 1976. The unemployment rates of women aged 17 to 24 were 11.2% in 2014 and 11.8% in 1976.
5. For a detailed analysis of youth labour market outcomes, see Galarneau, Morissette and Usalcas (2013) and Bernard (2013).
6. As will be shown below, the drop in the full-time employment rate of men aged 55 to 64 from the mid-1970s to the mid-1990s resulted mainly from falling labour market participation. Subsequently, the participation rate and full-time employment rate of this group increased. See Schirle (2008) for an analysis of the factors underlying the rise in labour force participation rates of men aged 55 to 64 since the mid-1990s.

Economic Insights, no. 049, July 2015 • Statistics Canada, Catalogue no. 11-626-X
Full-time Employment, 1976 to 2014

ECONOMIC INSIGHTS   3

Table 2
Percentage of population employed full time in their main job, by age group and sex, 1976 to 2014

	Percentage of men employed full time as		Percentage of women employed full time as	
	Employees	Employees or self-employed	Employees	Employees or self-employed
	percent			
Population aged 17 to 24				
1976	73.0	76.8	57.2	58.7
1997	58.7	62.3	43.7	45.6
2007	64.8	67.6	53.6	54.9
2014	56.8	59.1	47.1	48.0
1976 to 2014	-16.2	-17.7	-10.2	-10.7
Population aged 25 to 29				
1976	81.2	89.1	42.5	44.3
1997	70.5	79.4	55.6	59.1
2007	74.1	82.8	64.7	68.3
2014	71.2	78.8	61.4	64.9
1976 to 2014	-10.1	-10.2	18.9	20.6
Population aged 30 to 54				
1976	74.7	90.0	33.0	36.1
1997	64.4	81.6	48.1	54.7
2007	67.5	84.0	57.1	64.1
2014	67.9	82.6	57.8	64.1
1976 to 2014	-6.8	-7.5	24.8	28.0
Population aged 55 to 64				
1976	56.8	70.2	20.3	22.8
1997	34.3	49.6	18.9	23.1
2007	40.8	56.9	30.8	36.3
2014	43.1	58.3	34.8	40.8
1976 to 2014	-13.6	-11.9	14.5	18.1

Note: The population consists of individuals who are not full-time students. Full-time employment is defined as working usually 30 hours or more per week. The main job is the job with the greatest number of weekly work hours.
Source: Statistics Canada, Labour Force Survey, 1976 to 2014.

Decomposing the trends: an accounting exercise

One way to shed light on this issue is to decompose changes in full-time employment rates into three components. In an accounting sense, the percentage of men employed full time may have dropped because proportionately: (a) fewer of them were participating in the labour market, i.e., were employed or actively looking for work; (b) fewer of those participating in the labour market were employed; and/or (c) more of those employed worked part time. In other words, men's full-time employment rate may have fallen because of a decline in their labour market participation rate, an increase in their unemployment rate, or an increase in the incidence of part-time employment.[7]

Table 3 quantifies the contribution of these three components. It shows that almost 40% of the decline in the full-time employment rate of men aged 30 to 54 observed from 1976 to 2014 was due to a decline in their labour force participation[8] while 41% was due to an increase in the relative importance of part-time employment. The remaining portion (almost 20%) was due, in an accounting sense, to increases in unemployment. Qualitatively similar findings hold for men aged 25 to 29 and 55 to 64.

In contrast, rising rates of labour force participation were the main factor behind the rise in the full-time employment rates of women aged 25 and over. Increasing labour force participation accounted for 85% of the increase in the full-time employment rate of women aged 30 to 54 observed from 1976 to 2014. The story was much the same among women aged 25 to 29 and 55 to 64.

Among youth, declines in the full-time employment rate were largely the result of the increasing incidence of part-time employment. This component contributed to almost three-quarters of the decline in full-time employment among men aged 17 to 24 and for more than the entire decline observed among young women. For young women, the downward pressure that rising part-time employment exerted on their full-time employment rate more than offset the upward pressure resulting from rising labour force participation.

A separate analysis of the 1976-to-1997 period and the 1997-to-2014 period reveals interesting patterns. As Table 2 and Chart 3 showed, the full-time employment rates of men aged 25 to 29 and of men aged 30 to 54 changed very little from 1997 to 2014. The same was true for men overall.[9] Second, changes in the labour market participation of men aged 55 to 64 accounted for about two-thirds of the substantial decline in their full-time employment rate from 1976 to 1997 and almost entirely for the more modest increase in their full-time employment rate afterwards. Declines in the participation rate of men aged 17 to 24 contributed to about half of the relatively small drop in their full-time employment rate from 1997 to 2014.

Considering the entire 1976-to-2014 period, declines in participation rates and in the incidence of full-time employment were the two main factors underlying the drop in men's full-time employment rates. Rising part-time employment drove the entire decline in the full-time employment rate of women aged 17 to 24. Because rising participation rates accounted for most of the increase in adult women's full-time employment rates from 1976 to 2014 and has been the subject of much scholarly research,[10] the remainder of this article focuses on the declines observed among men and youth.

---

7. Full-time employment rates are the product of three components: (1) the ratio of full-time employment to total employment, (2) the ratio of total employment to the labour force (one minus the unemployment rate); and (3) the labour force / population ratio (the participation rate). Taking the logarithm of full-time employment rates and first-differencing the resulting logarithmic values yields an additive decomposition of the percentage change in full-time employment rates into the (first-differenced logarithmic values of the) three aforementioned components.
8. Strictly speaking, the numbers in Table 3 account for the percentage change in full-time employment rates observed from 1976 to 2014. For instance, the full-time employment rate of men aged 30 to 54 fell from 90.0% in 1976 to 82.6% in 2014. This drop of roughly 7.5 percentage points (after accounting for rounding) represents an 8.3% decline (i.e., 7.5% divided by 90.0%). The numbers in Table 3 account for this 8.3% decline.
9. For this reason, decompositions of changes in the full-time employment rates of these groups from 1997 to 2014 are not meaningful.
10. For a review of this research, see Goldin (2006).

Chart 2
Changes in the percentage of population employed full time in their main job, by sex and age group, 1976 to 2014

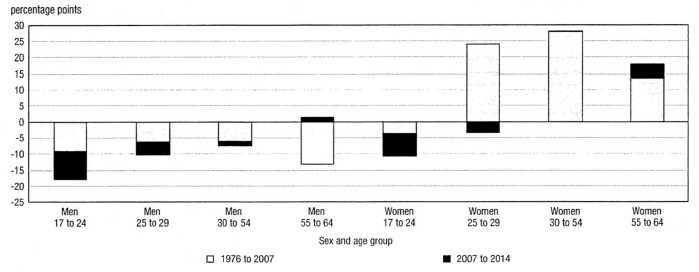

Note: The population consists of individuals who are not full-time students. Full-time employment is defined as working usually 30 hours or more per week. The main job is the job with the greatest number of weekly work hours.
Source: Statistics Canada, Labour Force Survey, 1976 to 2014.

Chart 3
Percentage of men employed full time in their main job, by age group, 1976 to 2014

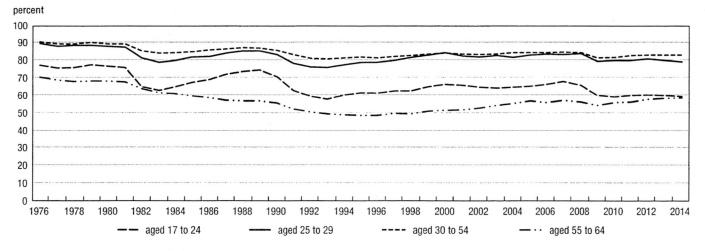

Note: Men who are not full-time students. Full-time employment is defined as working usually 30 hours or more per week. The main job is the job with the greatest number of weekly work hours.
Source: Statistics Canada, Labour Force Survey, 1976 to 2014.

Compositional changes

The socio-demographic characteristics of men in Canada changed considerably since the mid-1970s. Their average age increased, potentially raising the prevalence of activity limitations and lowering labour market participation.[11] However, they also obtained higher levels of education —a trend that might have increased their likelihood of being employed full time. They also became more likely to have an employed spouse, and their distribution across provinces changed as economic activity shifted towards the oil-producing provinces of Alberta, Saskatchewan, and Newfoundland and Labrador. To estimate the extent to which such changes might have affected men's full-time employment rates, multivariate analyses were conducted.[12]

11. The decline over time in the relative importance of physically demanding occupations may have had an opposite effect.
12. Data from 1976 and 2014 were pooled. A binary indicator for whether an individual was employed full time was regressed on the following variables: a quadratic term in age; being permanently unable to work; having a university degree; being self-employed; being married and having a spouse who is (a) not employed (b) employed part time (c) employed full time (d) permanently unable to work (e) a university graduate; number of children; province of residence; and a binary indicator for 2014.

Economic Insights, no. 049, July 2015 • Statistics Canada, Catalogue no. 11-626-X
Full-time Employment, 1976 to 2014

Table 3
Accounting for changes in full-time employment rates from 1976 to 2014

	1976 to 2014		1976 to 1997		1997 to 2014	
	Men	Women	Men	Women	Men	Women
	percent					
Individuals aged 17 to 24						
Percentage change in full-time employment rate	-23.1	-18.2	-18.9	-22.2	-5.1	5.2
Proportion due to changes in:						
Participation	23.8	-58.1	15.0	-30.0	58.6	81.6
Unemployment	3.7	-3.3	14.0	13.8	-37.4	81.8
Part-time employment	72.5	161.3	71.0	116.2	78.8	-63.4
Total	100.0	100.0	100.0	100.0	100.0	100.0
Individuals aged 25 to 29						
Percentage change in full-time employment rate	-11.5	46.5	-10.8	33.4	-0.7	9.8
Proportion due to changes in:						
Participation	35.7	97.9	22.0	116.0	...	42.1
Unemployment	21.7	6.3	40.1	0.5	...	24.3
Part-time employment	42.5	-4.2	37.9	-16.5	...	33.6
Total	100.0	100.0	100.0	100.0	...	100.0
Individuals aged 30 to 54						
Percentage change in full-time employment rate	-8.3	77.4	-9.3	51.4	1.1	17.1
Proportion due to changes in:						
Participation	39.5	85.2	30.7	101.4	...	42.6
Unemployment	19.7	1.9	39.2	-3.2	...	15.4
Part-time employment	40.8	12.9	30.2	1.8	...	42.1
Total	100.0	100.0	100.0	100.0	...	100.0
Individuals aged 55 to 64						
Percentage change in full-time employment rate	-17.0	79.3	-29.3	1.6	17.4	76.5
Proportion due to changes in:						
Participation	45.5	107.0	68.9	...	96.0	82.8
Unemployment	15.4	-1.5	10.8	...	5.5	4.1
Part-time employment	39.1	-5.5	20.3	...	-1.5	13.1
Total	100.0	100.0	100.0	...	100.0	100.0
Individuals aged 17 to 64						
Percentage change in full-time employment rate	-12.0	42.9	-11.6	23.5	-0.5	15.7
Proportion due to changes in:						
Participation	48.5	102.1	41.4	137.3	...	51.1
Unemployment	6.7	6.2	22.7	-2.1	...	18.2
Part-time employment	44.8	-8.3	35.9	-35.2	...	30.7
Total	100.0	100.0	100.0	100.0	...	100.0

... not applicable
Note: Changes in full-time employment rates for individuals who are not full-time students. Full-time employment rates equal the percentage of individuals usually working 30 hours or more per week as employees or self-employed workers in their main job. The main job is the job with the greatest number of weekly hours of work. Sources of change may not add to 100.0 because of rounding.
Source: Statistics Canada, Labour Force Survey, 1976 and 2014.

The results show that, of the 7.5-percentage-point decline in the full-time employment rate observed among men aged 30 to 54 from 1976 to 2014, 6.1 percentage points remain once changes in socio-demographic characteristics are taken into account. In other words, approximately four-fifths of the decline in the full-time employment rate of men aged 30 to 54 remain unexplained and thus, are due to factors that are not measured in the Labour Force Survey (LFS).[13]

The deterioration in labour market outcomes of immigrant men is one potential factor that may have exerted downward pressure on the full-time employment rate of men overall. This possibility cannot be assessed using the LFS because immigration status is only available on that survey since 2006. Census data from 1981 to 2006 show that the full-time employment rate of immigrant men aged 30 to 54 fell by 7 to 14 percentage points, depending on their duration of residence in Canada.[14] However, the drop in the full-time employment rate was not limited to immigrant men as census data also show that Canadian-born men in that age group experienced a 4-percentage-point decline in their full-time employment rate over that period. This decline is very similar to the 5-percentage-point drop observed among men aged 30 to 54 overall.[15] Hence, the deterioration in labour market outcomes observed among immigrant men only partly accounts for the broader decline in full-time employment.

As was the case for men aged 30 to 54, changes in socio-economic characteristics were not key factors underlying the declines in full-time employment rates of youth. All of the drop in the full-time employment rate of men aged 17 to 24 (again excluding full-time students) remains when socio-demographic characteristics are taken into account. This is also the case among women in that age group. Among men aged 25 to 29, changes in socio-demographic characteristics account for about 2 percentage points of the 10.2-percentage-point decline in the full-time employment rate—or about 20%. In sum, compositional effects were not the main drivers behind the decline in the full-time employment rates of men under 55.

Labour force participation

Whether one considers men aged 17 to 24, 25 to 29, or 30 to 54, at least two-thirds—and sometimes almost all—of the decline in labour force participation observed from 1976 to 2014 remains after controlling for the aforementioned socio-economic characteristics (excluding the self-employment indicator).[16] This suggests that other factors played an important role.

---

13. An alternative approach is to focus on the full-time employment rate of men aged 30 to 54 who are not permanently unable to work, which fell by 6.6 percentage points from 1976 to 2014. Once changes in socio-economic characteristics are taken into account, a decline of 6.2 percentage points remains for this group.

14. These full-time employment rates are based on actual hours worked at all jobs during the census reference week. Along with individuals who attended school (part time or full time) in the nine months prior to the reference week, employed individuals who were absent from work during that week are excluded from the calculation of these rates. Conceptually comparable data from the LFS from the month of May and from the Census of Population show that the full-time employment rate of (the entire population of) men aged 30 to 54 fell by between 5.2 and 5.7 percentage points from 1981 to 2006.

15. Census data show that the full-time employment rate of all men aged 30 to 54 dropped from 86.9% in 1981 to 81.7% in 2006. The corresponding percentages for Canadian-born men in the same age group are 85.8% and 81.8%. Using the National Household Survey (NHS) to extend the observation period yields full-time employment rates for 2011 that equal 80.7% for all men aged 30 to 54 and 81.2% for those born in Canada.

16. From 1976 to 2014, the participation rates of these groups fell by 6 percentage points, 4 percentage points and 3 percentage points, respectively.

Chart 4
Changes in real median hourly wages in full-time jobs and changes in labour force participation rates from 1981 to 2014, by age group, education, and region — Men aged 17 to 54

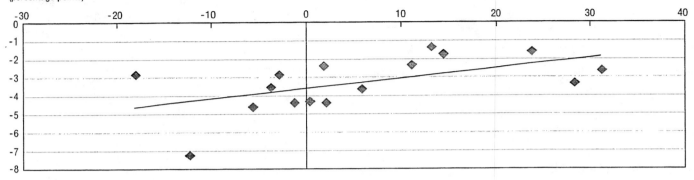

Note: Changes in participation rates of men aged 17 to 54 who are not full-time students are correlated, over the 1981-to-2014 period, with percentage changes in real median hourly wages of men aged 17 to 54 employed full time. Data are grouped by age groups (17 to 24; 25 to 34; 35 to 44; 45 to 54), education (having a university degree or not), and region (oil-producing provinces and other provinces), thereby yielding 16 observations. Oil-producing provinces include Alberta, Saskatchewan as well as Newfoundland and Labrador.
Sources: Statistics Canada, Survey of Work History of 1981 and Labour Force Survey, 1981 and 2014.

Changes in the wage structure are potentially one of these factors. From the early 1980s to 2014, real wages grew at a different pace across age groups, education levels, and regions. For instance, men aged 17 to 24 with no university degree, living in the oil-producing provinces of Alberta, Saskatchewan, and Newfoundland and Labrador and employed full time earned very similar real median hourly wages in 1981 and 2014. In contrast, their counterparts living in other provinces saw their real median hourly wages drop by 12% during that period. Since lower wages makes labour market participation relatively less attractive, one would expect groups of men who experienced the sharpest declines in median wages during the 1981-to-2014 period to display the largest decrease in participation.

This is what happened. Grouping the data by age, education level, and region shows that changes in men's participation rates were positively correlated with changes in their real median wages during that period (Chart 4). Specifically, a 10% decline in real median hourly wages was associated with a 1-percentage-point decline in labour market participation.[17] While a thorough assessment of the degree to which changes in the wage structure reduced men's participation requires formal econometric analyses, the evidence shown in Chart 4 suggests that such changes contributed to reducing the participation rate of some men aged under 55.

Preferences for part-time work

Changes in work-hour preferences, for instance the increased demand for part-time employment, are another potential explanation for the decline in full-time employment rates, particularly among youth, men aged 25 to 29 and men aged 30 to 54. Analyses of whether or not this is the case must take account of the fact that the questions used to define involuntary part-time work changed with the re-design of the LFS in 1997. As a result, comparable concepts of involuntary part-time work are available within two periods: 1976 to 1995 and 1997 to 2014.[18] The examination of these two periods suggests that both an increase in involuntary part-time employment and growing preferences for part-time work played a role.

The first point to note is that most of the growth—between 71% and 84%—in the incidence of part-time employment observed since the mid-1970s took place during the 1976-to-1995 period.[19] During that period, growing involuntary part-time work was a dominant factor, generally accounting for at least three-quarters of the growth in the incidence of part-time employment among youth and men aged 25 to 54. For instance, of the 13-percentage-point increase in part-time employment experienced by employed men aged 17 to 24 from 1976 to 1995, 10 percentage points—or over 75% of the increase—were

---

17. This finding results from regressing the group-level changes in participation rates shown in Chart 4 on a constant term and percentage changes in real median hourly wages, using the mean population of each group in 1981 and 2014 as weights.
18. The introduction of the new concept of involuntary part-time work in September 1996 resulted in a break in the initial series during that year. Prior to September 1996, the reason for working part time was asked of all individuals whose total usual hours in all jobs were below 30 per week. Subsequently, this information was collected for all individuals who worked less than 30 hours per week at their main job or only job. Under the revised questionnaire, workers are defined as being involuntarily employed part time if they respond that: (a) they want to work 30 hours or more per week, and (b) the main reason for working less than 30 hours per week is "business conditions" or "could not find work with 30 or more hours," whether or not they looked for work with 30 or more hours per week during the past four weeks. Under the old questionnaire, workers were defined as being involuntarily employed part time if they responded that they "could only find part-time work."
19. The percentage of employed men aged 17 to 24 working part time in their main job grew from 4% in 1976 to 17% in 1995 and from 17% in 1997 to 21% in 2014. The percentage of employed women aged 17 to 24 working part time rose from 10% in 1976 to 30% in 1995 and from 33% in 1997 to 35% in 2014. Employed men aged 30 to 54 experienced more modest increases in part-time employment: the percentage working part time grew from 1% in 1976 to 4% in 1995 and from 4% in 1997 to 5% in 2014. Very similar patterns were observed among employed men aged 25 to 29.

Economic Insights, no. 049, July 2015 • Statistics Canada, Catalogue no. 11-626-X
Full-time Employment, 1976 to 2014

Table 4
Sources of increase in part-time employment among employed workers, selected age groups

Increase in part-time employment	Men aged				Women aged
	17 to 24	25 to 29	30 to 54	55 to 64	17 to 24
	percentage points				
From 1976 to 1995					
Involuntary part-time employment	10.0	3.6	1.9	2.4	15.3
Voluntary part-time employment	3.2	0.7	0.7	3.5	4.2
Total	13.2	4.3	2.6	5.9	19.5
From 1997 to 2014					
Involuntary part-time employment	-0.5	0.0	-0.1	0.4	-2.1
Voluntary part-time employment	3.9	0.8	0.7	-0.2	4.2
Total	3.4	0.8	0.6	0.2	2.1

Note: The concepts of involuntary and voluntary part-time employment used from 1976 to 1995 differ from those used from 1997 onwards. For this reason, numbers from the 1976-to-1995 period cannot be summed with those of the 1997-to-2014 period. Numbers are shown for women aged 17 to 24 and men aged 17 to 64, groups for which changes in the incidence of part-time employment account for a large proportion of the changes in full-time employment rates observed from 1976 to 2014.
Source: Labour Force Survey, 1976, 1995, 1997 and 2014.

due to higher involuntary part-time employment (Table 4). The corresponding numbers for employed women aged 17 to 24 are 20 percentage points and 15 percentage points, respectively. The important role played by involuntary part-time employment during that period is consistent with the fact that the Canadian labour market was fairly weak several years after the 1990-1992 recession.[20]

The story was different from 1997 to 2014. Among men under 55 and women aged 17 to 24, the entire growth in part-time employment during that period resulted from voluntary part-time work. However, part-time employment grew relatively little during that period.

Regional differences

The hypothesis that changes in employment preferences have driven the decline in full-time employment among men and youth is also belied by the regional dimension of these trends. In the oil-producing provinces of Alberta, Saskatchewan as well as Newfoundland and Labrador, the full-time employment rate of men aged 30 to 54 declined by 3.0 percentage points between 1976 and 2014 compared with a decline of 8.4 percentage points in other provinces (Table 5). Similarly, among men aged 25 to 29, the rate declined by 4.3 percentage points in oil-producing provinces compared with 11.7 percentage points elsewhere. Among women aged 17 to 24, the full-time employment rate fell marginally in oil-producing provinces but declined by 12.6 percentage points elsewhere. Many of these regional

differences hold when the data are further disaggregated by education level (Table 6). It appears unlikely that employment preferences towards part-time work changed so dramatically along these regional lines. Instead, differences in labour demand growth across provinces likely drove much of the changes in the full-time employment rates of these groups.[21] Both in oil-producing provinces and in other provinces, declines in labour force participation rates and increases in the incidence of part-time employment accounted for at least 90% of the overall decline in men's full-time employment rates (Table 7).

Summary

Although the percentage of Canadians employed full time has risen modestly over the last four decades, this change masks diverging trends across sexes, age groups, and regions. Women aged 25 and over have massively increased their presence in the ranks of the Canadian workforce employed full time. In contrast, men of all ages, especially those under 25 in the non-oil-producing provinces, have experienced a decline in their full-time employment rates. Women under 25 living in these provinces were also employed full time in smaller proportions in 2014 than their counterparts were in 1976.

The evidence gathered in this article does not support the conjecture that the decline in the full-time employment rates of men and of youth resulted simply from growing preferences for part-time employment. Instead, it shows that, for these groups, much of the increase in the incidence of part-time employment was generally involuntary, i.e., reflected the willingness to work full time and the inability to find full-time employment. The study also showed that the decline in men's full-time employment rates cannot be explained solely by the deterioration in employment opportunities of immigrant men.

While the increase in the full-time employment rates of women aged 25 and over was driven almost entirely by the growing participation rates of these women, the decline in men's rates of full-time employment came from numerous sources. Rising part-time employment as well as—for men aged 25 and over—increases in inactivity contributed significantly to the drop in the proportion of men employed full time. Increases in unemployment generally did not play a primary role, although they did account for some of the changes in full-time employment rates. In fact, some groups—for example, men and women aged 17 to 24—had substantially lower full-time employment rates in 2014 than in 1976 even though their unemployment rates during these two years were fairly similar. This fact is an important reminder that aggregate measures sometimes do not provide a complete picture and that rigorous assessments of the degree of success of people in the Canadian labour market require considering jointly numerous labour market indicators.

---

20. For instance, the unemployment rate of men aged 25 to 54 averaged 8.7% in 1995, compared with 6.3% in 1989 (CANSIM Table 282-0002).
21. These regional differences do not simply reflect the strong employment growth observed in Alberta during the 2000s. From 2001 to 2008—a period during which oil prices received by Canada's oil producers more than doubled (Morissette, Chan, and Lu 2015)—the full-time employment rates of youth and men aged 25 to 54 increased faster in Newfoundland and Labrador and Saskatchewan than they did in non-oil-producing provinces, considered collectively.

Table 5
Percentage of population employed full time in their main job (as employees or self-employed), by age group, sex and region, 1976 to 2014

	Men aged				Women aged			
	17 to 24	25 to 29	30 to 54	55 to 64	17 to 24	25 to 29	30 to 54	55 to 64
	percent							
Oil-producing provinces								
1976	81.4	89.9	90.5	71.1	58.3	39.7	34.6	23.7
2007	77.8	88.6	88.4	65.2	63.1	66.2	64.1	42.0
2014	72.5	85.6	87.5	65.9	56.6	65.8	62.6	44.5
1976 to 2014	-8.9	-4.3	-3.0	-5.3	-1.6	26.1	28.0	20.9
Other provinces								
1976	75.9	88.9	90.0	70.0	58.7	45.1	36.4	22.6
2007	65.2	81.6	83.2	55.5	53.1	68.7	64.1	35.4
2014	56.2	77.2	81.5	56.9	46.1	64.7	64.4	40.2
1976 to 2014	-19.8	-11.7	-8.4	-13.1	-12.6	19.7	28.0	17.6

Note: The population consists of individuals who are not full-time students. Full-time employment is defined as working usually 30 hours or more per week. The main job is the job with the greatest number of weekly work hours. Oil-producing provinces include Alberta, Saskatchewan, and Newfoundland and Labrador.
Source: Statistics Canada, Labour Force Survey, 1976 to 2014.

Table 6
Percentage of population employed full time in their main job (as employees or self-employed), by age group, sex, education and region, 1976 to 2014

	Men aged				Women aged			
	17 to 24	25 to 29	30 to 54	55 to 64	17 to 24	25 to 29	30 to 54	55 to 64
	percent							
Individuals with no university degree								
Oil-producing provinces								
1976	80.8	88.6	89.6	70.4	57.3	36.4	33.5	22.7
2007	77.4	87.7	87.4	64.4	61.8	61.5	62.6	41.4
2014	72.3	84.8	86.3	65.7	54.9	59.3	60.3	44.5
1976 to 2014	-8.6	-3.8	-3.4	-4.7	-2.4	22.8	26.7	21.8
Other provinces								
1976	75.6	88.4	89.2	69.0	58.0	42.4	35.5	22.0
2007	64.6	80.3	81.4	53.9	51.5	64.5	61.4	33.5
2014	55.2	75.7	79.8	55.4	44.0	59.3	60.9	38.8
1976 to 2014	-20.4	-12.7	-9.4	-13.5	-13.9	16.9	25.4	16.7
All provinces								
1976	76.4	88.4	89.3	69.2	57.9	41.6	35.3	22.1
2007	67.0	81.6	82.4	55.4	53.5	64.0	61.6	34.5
2014	58.3	77.5	80.9	57.1	46.0	59.3	60.8	39.6
1976 to 2014	-18.1	-10.9	-8.3	-12.1	-11.9	17.7	25.6	17.5
Individuals with a university degree								
Oil-producing provinces								
1976	F	F	97.2	F	F	F	F	F
2007	F	F	92.0	68.4	F	78.5	69.2	45.1
2014	F	88.2	91.4	66.5	F	77.8	68.0	44.9
1976 to 2014	F	F	-5.8	F	F	F	F	F
Other provinces								
1976	84.7	91.5	95.2	82.7	76.6	66.6	50.6	39.6
2007	75.5	86.1	88.6	60.6	65.7	77.5	71.6	44.1
2014	68.4	81.3	86.0	61.6	59.1	74.1	71.6	45.5
1976 to 2014	-16.3	-10.2	-9.2	-21.1	-17.5	7.5	21.0	6.0
All provinces								
1976	86.1	92.2	95.5	82.9	76.9	66.1	50.5	40.8
2007	76.9	87.0	89.0	61.5	67.3	77.7	71.3	44.2
2014	69.5	82.5	86.8	62.3	60.7	74.8	71.1	45.4
1976 to 2014	-16.6	-9.6	-8.6	-20.6	-16.2	8.7	20.5	4.6

F too unreliable to be published
Note: The population consists of individuals who are not full-time students. Full-time employment is defined as working usually 30 hours or more per week. The main job is the job with the greatest number of weekly work hours. Oil-producing provinces include Alberta, Saskatchewan, and Newfoundland and Labrador.
Source: Statistics Canada, Labour Force Survey, 1976 to 2014.

Table 7
Accounting for changes in full-time employment rates from 1976 to 2014, by sex and region

	Men		Women	
	Other provinces	Oil-producing provinces	Other provinces	Oil-producing provinces
	percent			
Individuals aged 17 to 24				
Percentage change in full-time employment rate	-26.0	-11.0	-21.5	-2.8
Proportion due to changes in:				
Participation	23.2	25.0	-47.4	...
Unemployment	5.2	-6.7	-3.0	...
Part-time employment	71.6	81.6	150.4	...
Total	100.0	100.0	100.0	...
Individuals aged 25 to 29				
Percentage change in full-time employment rate	-13.2	-4.8	43.7	65.8
Proportion due to changes in:				
Participation	35.3	30.5	102.2	82.5
Unemployment	22.6	22.8	6.5	3.3
Part-time employment	42.1	46.6	-8.7	14.3
Total	100.0	100.0	100.0	100.0
Individuals aged 30 to 54				
Percentage change in full-time employment rate	-9.4	-3.3	77.1	80.9
Proportion due to changes in:				
Participation	40.3	22.3	86.1	78.6
Unemployment	19.6	30.2	2.4	-1.2
Part-time employment	40.0	47.5	11.5	22.5
Total	100.0	100.0	100.0	100.0
Individuals aged 55 to 64				
Percentage change in full-time employment rate	-18.8	-7.4	77.6	88.2
Proportion due to changes in:				
Participation	47.4	18.5	108.3	99.9
Unemployment	13.8	39.7	-1.5	-1.9
Part-time employment	38.8	41.8	-6.8	1.9
Total	100.0	100.0	100.0	100.0
Individuals aged 17 to 64				
Percentage change in full-time employment rate	-13.6	-5.1	41.8	49.2
Proportion due to changes in:				
Participation	48.6	40.4	103.9	92.9
Unemployment	7.5	5.2	6.9	1.7
Part-time employment	43.9	54.4	-10.8	5.4
Total	100.0	100.0	100.0	100.0

... not applicable
Note: Changes in full-time employment rates for individuals who are not full-time students. Full-time employment rates equal the percentage of individuals usually working 30 hours or more per week as employees or self-employed workers in their main job. The main job is the job with the greatest number of weekly hours of work. Sources of change may not add to 100.0 because of rounding. Oil-producing provinces include Alberta, Saskatchewan, and Newfoundland and Labrador.
Source: Statistics Canada, Labour Force Survey, 1976 and 2014.

References

Bernard, A. 2013. *Unemployment Dynamics Among Canada's Youth.* Economic Insights, no. 24. Statistics Canada Catalogue no 11-626-X. Ottawa: Statistics Canada.

Galarneau, D., R. Morissette, and J. Usalcas. 2013. "What has changed for young people in Canada?" *Insights on Canadian Society.* Statistics Canada Catalogue no. 75-006-X. Ottawa: Statistics Canada.

Goldin, C. 2006. "The quiet revolution that transformed women's employment, education, and family." *American Economic Review* 96 (2): 1–21.

Morissette, R., P.C.W. Chan, and Y. Lu. 2015. "Wages, youth employment and school enrollment: Recent evidence from increases in world oil prices." *Journal of Human Resources* 50 (1): 222–253.

Schirle, T. 2008. "Why have the labor force participation rates of older men increased since the mid–1990s?" *Journal of Labor Economics* 26 (4): 549–594.

Statistics Canada. 2010. *Guide to the Labour Force Survey 2010.* Statistics Canada Catalogue no. 71-543-G. Ottawa: Statistics Canada.

Economica

A Shred of Credible Evidence on the Long-run Elasticity of Labour Supply

By Orley Ashenfelter†, Kirk Doran‡ and Bruce Schaller††

†*Princeton University* ‡*University of Notre Dame*
††*New York City Department of Transportation*

Final version received 29 January 2010.

All public policies regarding taxation and the redistribution of income rely on assumptions about the long-run effect of wages rates on labour supply. The variation in existing estimates calls for a simple, natural experiment in which men can change their hours of work, and in which wages have been exogenously and permanently changed. We use a panel dataset of taxi drivers who choose their own hours, and who experienced two exogenous permanent fare increases, and estimate an elasticity of labour supply of -0.2, implying that income effects dominate substitution effects in the long-run labour supply of males.

Introduction

The effect of wage rates on long-run labour supply is a key ingredient in the discussion of virtually all public policies regarding taxation, social safety nets and the redistribution of income. Although there is a relatively broad consensus that the long-run elasticity of labour supply is not likely to be large, especially for adult males, this consensus is a result of many individual studies that face a litany of familiar limitations.[1] The two most serious problems in studying worker preferences between income and leisure that modern studies face are (a) the inability of most workers to alter their hours of work without changing jobs, and (b) the consequent inability of the analyst to measure exogenous changes in wages that workers face. Our goal in this paper is to provide a straightforward analysis of the labour supply of workers whose hours are flexible in response to an exogenous wage increase. To do this we have deliberately selected data for a group where a transparent econometric analysis is feasible, rather than applying more complex methods to a broad-based and representative dataset. Needless to say, our approach has the obvious advantage of transparency, while suffering from the disadvantage that it may not be appropriate to generalize our findings to other populations.

Our analysis relies on a new panel dataset of New York City taxi drivers who choose their own work hours, and who experienced two exogenous, permanent increases in their real wages. New York taxi drivers either own or lease taxi 'medallions', which give them the right to collect passengers when hailed on the street, subject to a number of rules and regulations, including the fees that they may charge. This economic environment provides a straightforward method for estimating the labour supply response to a wage change, if one occurs. Our data indicate that work responses to exogenous increases in the fare structure are small, and negative. Worker wages, on the other hand, are strongly affected by increases in the fare structure. Taken together, the evidence implies that the long-run uncompensated elasticity of labour supply lies around -0.2, and that it may be estimated in our data with considerable precision.

Taxi drivers have been the subject of several studies that attempt to use the time series behaviour of individual drivers who face stable fare structures to study intertemporal substitution and reference dependence in driver preferences (see Farber 2005 and the references therein). However, absent the observation of exogenous, permanent wage

© The London School of Economics and Political Science 2010

changes, these papers cannot measure long-run labour supply parameters and they do not attempt to do so.

In the next section of the paper we provide a brief discussion of the New York City taxi industry. We then introduce our new dataset on taxi revenues and fares, set out a simple theoretical model of taxi driver incentives, and discuss the empirical results. The final section contains some brief concluding remarks and indicates some of the implications of our findings for future research.

I. TAXIS IN NEW YORK

There are five main types of taxis in New York City: yellow taxis, car services, black cars, limousines, and illegal so-called gitney cabs.[2] Only yellow taxis are legally allowed to accept passengers from street hails, and this—along with hails from passengers waiting in lines at airports, train stations, and hotels—is the only legal source of passengers for yellow taxis. All taxi and livery services are regulated by the New York City Taxi and Limousine Commission (TLC).

In 2006, there were 12,779 yellow taxis in New York City, out of a total of about 46,000 legal taxi, car service and black car vehicles. The yellow taxis concentrate on serving Manhattan residents, who are transported in 71% of their trips. As of 2002, 'two-thirds of Manhattan residents used cabs for work and/or personal trips at least some of the time', and overall, 'Manhattan adults hail a cab an average of 100 times a year' (Schaller 2006). In turn, '90% of all taxi trips originate in Manhattan' (Schaller 2006). Yellow taxis are thus an important part of the Manhattan transportation system, with '8.5 yellow ... taxis per 1000 Manhattan residents in 2005' (Schaller 2006).

The only way to legally drive a yellow taxi is with a taxi licence: 'a painted aluminum medallion ... which is affixed to the hood of every yellow ... cab' (Schaller 2006). The number of medallions is determined by the TLC, and has not varied much from around 12,000 for the past 60 years. There are three main ways to get access to a medallion: (1) buying one on the open market; (2) renting one for long-term periods of time as a 'named driver'; and (3) renting a medallion one shift at a time as an 'unnamed driver'. Individually-owned taxis are now required to 'be driven 210 shifts per year by the medallion owner, for licenses transferred since 1990', although there is some question about whether the required number of shifts is enforced (Schaller 2006).

The TLC also sets the fares that taxis must charge. A taxi trip begins with a fare drop: a large charge that is accrued as soon as the taxi drives for more than a short distance (this distance has ranged from one-seventh to one-fifth of a mile since 1952). After this, the passengers are charged for mileage (when the taxi is moving at more than 12 mph) and wait time (when the taxi is stopped or moving at less than 12 mph). Finally, there are and have been various surcharges for trips beginning during certain times of the day, and various flat fares for trips to and/or from specific airports.

Since July 1952, the TLC has changed the fares 13 times. In nominal dollars, the fare drop has increased from $0.25 to $2.50 for the first fifth of a mile, the charge per mile has increased from $0.20 to $2.00, and the charge per minute has increased from $0.03 to $0.40. Average fares have increased from $0.83 to $9.61.

The recent fare increases analysed in this paper (March 1996 and May 2004) have resulted in increased total revenue per hour (i.e. the number of passengers hailing taxis did not decline enough to offset additional revenue from higher fares per trip), which suggests that the demand for taxis is inelastic. It is possible to interpret some of these fare

© The London School of Economics and Political Science 2010

increases as accounting for inflation; however, after the 2004 fare increase, drivers' real cash incomes exceeded 'driver incomes in 1929 for the first time since the Crash' (Schaller 2006). This suggests that there have been long-term changes in drivers' real net hourly wages that have been precipitated in part by nominal fare changes instituted by the TLC.

In the next section, we discuss the data that we use to analyse the response of taxi drivers to two changes in real revenue per mile that were brought about by the 1996 and 2004 fare increases.

II. DATA

The TLC inspects each yellow taxi three times a year at its central inspection facility. The data used in this paper are from the TLC's complete set of official inspection records from September 1994 to December 2005. Each inspection record includes the medallion number, the registered type of driving arrangement (owner–driver, owner–driver with another driver, named driver or unnamed driver), the odometer reading, the taximeter reading, and the date of the inspection. From these data, we can calculate the number of days since the last inspection (always about 4 months), the month in which the inspection took place (to capture seasonal effects), the number of miles driven since the last inspection, and the revenue earned since the last inspection.

The measure of labour supply that we construct from these data is the number of miles driven. With a constant average speed (which we take to be driver-specific in the analysis below), miles driven is a good measure of hours worked, and thus of labour supply. However, it should be clear that although hours worked and miles driven are highly related, they are not identical. The primary difference will be due to waiting time that results in passenger revenue but does not result from miles being driven. We suspect that the primary place where this happens is where taxis are waiting in a line at an airport or a hotel, for the purpose of shuttling passengers between the two. However, as of 1990, only 4% of all yellow taxi trips began or ended in La Guardia or Kennedy airports; the number at Newark airport was negligible (Schaller 2006). This implies that most taxi drivers are probably cruising on Manhattan streets when they are looking for a passenger, so that miles driven and hours worked will be closely related.[3]

The corresponding real net revenue earned per mile driven in a given four-month period is the real revenue earned during that period minus the real costs, divided by the number of miles driven. We use as our measure of the real earnings from driving a mile the real revenues divided by the number of miles driven. Holding velocity and real costs constant, the average real revenue per mile is proportional to the average hourly wage. In the interest of holding real costs—which we presume are primarily fixed—constant, we exclude from our sample all medallions that are being leased by their drivers (named drivers and unnamed drivers), since real lease rates change over time.

Since we are interested in estimating the labour supply of taxi drivers, not of taxis, we would like each observation to be for a particular driver. To help to achieve this, we also exclude from our sample any medallion owned by a driver who rents out his medallion to another driver for the complementary shifts. Finally, we exclude from our dataset records in which the inspection took place more than 365 days before one of the fare increases, records in which the inspection took place less than four months after one of the fare increases (this eliminates inspection periods that straddle both sides of the fare increase), and records in which the inspection took place more than four months plus 365 days after a fare increase.

We are left with a total of 19,134 observations (inspections) of 2637 medallions, where each medallion at any point in time is driven by an individual owner–driver.[4]

© The London School of Economics and Political Science 2010

640   ECONOMICA   [OCTOBER

These observations cover the labour supplied by these drivers over the following periods: from 1 March 1995 to 9 February 1996; from 1 July 1996 to 1 July 1997; from 12 May 2003 to 3 May 2004; and from 7 September 2004 to 7 September 2005. Our data cover an average of 825 days for each medallion, with a standard deviation of 368 days.

We do not know with certainty that each observation represents the work of one driver, since the driver associated with a medallion at the beginning of an inspection period may have sold his medallion before the next inspection. We also do not know for sure that the driver associated with a medallion in one year is necessarily the same driver associated with that medallion in another year. However, we do know the total number of taxi medallion sales each month from January 1990 to December 2005. On average, only 18 exchanges of privately-owned medallions occur each month, meaning that within the average inspection period, less than 3% of medallions change hands. Some of these should actually involve sales to corporations that lease medallions, thus removing drivers from our sample, not matching new drivers to existing medallions. Our medallion fixed effects are thus only a proxy for driver-level fixed effects. Since at most 3% of these medallions changed hands in any given period, most medallions must have stayed in the hands of the same owner–drivers during the short periods of time before and after each fare change, which implies that our primary analysis should not be affected.

We report summary statistics from these data in Table 1, and a very simple pre-post analysis of differences in miles driven and revenue received per mile in Table 2a (the full panel) and Table 2b (a balanced subset of the full panel). The basic data surrounding the fare structure increases are also reported in Figures 1 and 2. It is clear from the figures that the real average revenue per mile was higher in the three years after each fare change than in the years before, suggesting that we can measure the labour supply response of owner–drivers to changes in real wages using the fare changes as an instrument. The figures also are consistent with only a small, and perhaps negative, permanent change in miles driven in response to the fare changes. Taken at face value, the simple division of the proportionate change in miles driven by the proportionate change in revenue per mile provides a measure of the uncompensated labour supply elasticity. For the balanced

TABLE 1

SIMPLE STATISTICS

Variable	Mean	St. dev.	Min.	Max.	Observations
By inspection					
Owner–driver? (1 = yes, 0 = no)	0.49	0.50	0	1	102,275
Days since last inspection	122	4	40	237	102,275
Miles driven since last inspection	15,989	6163	4000	41,997	102,275
Miles driven per day	131	50	24	408	102,275
Revenue earned since last inspection	$21,597	$8465	$3007	$68,536	67,317
Revenue earned per day	$177	$69	$25	$553	67,317
Revenue earned per mile (a measure of the wage)	$0.68	$0.14	$0.33	$1.41	65,888
Real revenue earned per mile (in December 2005 dollars)	$0.81	$0.14	$0.44	$1.56	49,112
By medallion					
Owner–driver? (1 = yes, 0 = no)	0.40	0.38	0	1	4658
Number of inspections	22	12	1	46	4658

© The London School of Economics and Political Science 2010

TABLE 2a

SIMPLE ESTIMATES OF LABOUR SUPPLY USING ALL OBSERVATIONS AND CONTROLLING FOR DRIVER HETEROGENEITY WITH FIXED EFFECTS

	Change in revenue per mile	Change in miles driven
Simple difference table: medallion fixed effects, no other controls		
1996 fare increase	+ $0.14 (+ 17%)	− 477 miles (− 3.2%)
2004 fare increase	+ $0.15 (+ 19%)	− 824 miles (− 5.6%)
Difference table: medallion fixed effects, controls for month and days since last inspection		
1996 fare increase	+ $0.14 (+ 17%)	− 399 miles (− 2.7%)
2004 fare increase	+ $0.15 (+ 19%)	− 818 miles (− 5.6%)

Notes

All changes are computed as the coefficient of a dummy variable indicating the year noted and are significant at the 0.1% level. Revenue is in December 2005 dollars. Miles driven measures the number of miles driven since the last inspection. The average number of days between inspections is 122 (4 months), with a standard deviation of 4 days. Since the panel is not fully balanced, these results are computed from a regression that includes medallion fixed effects in order to use all the data.

The regressions in the last two rows also contain a variable measuring the number of days since the taxi was last inspected.

TABLE 2b

SIMPLE ESTIMATES OF LABOUR SUPPLY USING ONLY OBSERVATIONS WITH CONTINUOUS PANEL DATA

	Change in revenue per mile	Change in miles driven
Simple difference table (balanced panel): no other controls		
1996 fare increase	+ $0.15*** (+ 19.2%)	− 819 miles* (− 5.6%)
2004 fare increase	+ $0.15*** (+ 20.9%)	− 764 miles** (− 5.1%)
Difference table: controls for month and days since last inspection		
1996 fare increase	+ $0.15*** (+ 19.0%)	− 758 miles* (− 5.2%)
2004 fare increase	+ $0.15*** (+ 20.9%)	− 758 miles** (− 5.1%)

Notes

***,**,*Indicate significant at the 0.1%, 1%, 10% level.

Revenue is in December 2005 dollars. Miles driven measures the number of miles driven since the last inspection. The average number of days between inspections is 122.6 with a standard deviation of 3.86 days in 1996, and 121.7 with a standard deviation of 2.08 days in 2004.

sample of data these estimates are all roughly − 5%/20% = − 0.25. As we shall see below, this is close to the estimate obtained from a more complete econometric analysis.

III. A SIMPLE MODEL OF BEHAVIOUR FOR TAXI DRIVER LABOUR SUPPLY

What is apparent from the previous discussion is that drivers do not face explicit wage rates, but instead face a taxi fare function that relates their income to hours worked through the miles they travel. A simple model of this behaviour starts with the standard assumption that a driver has utility function

(1) $u = u(h, y),$

© The London School of Economics and Political Science 2010

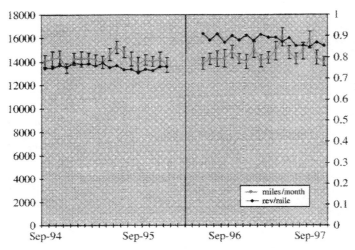

FIGURE 1. How the March 1996 fare change affected real revenue per mile and miles driven.

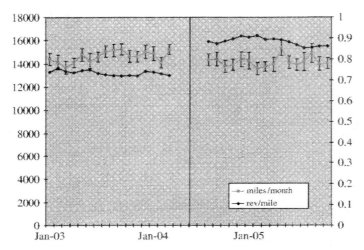

FIGURE 2. How the May 2004 fare change affected real revenue per mile and miles driven.

where h is hours worked and y is income from driving, and $u_h < 0$, $u_y > 0$. A worker also faces a schedule relating work to income

(2) $y = g(h; \theta)$,

where θ represents the parametric part of the fare structure. The driver optimizes by working at a point where

(3) $-u_h/u_y = g_h$,

i.e. the rate of substitution of leisure for goods equals the marginal effect of hours on income.

A convenient parameterization to the rate of substitution function $-u_h/u_y$ is $-u_h/u_y = \alpha h^\beta$, while $g(h;\theta) = \theta h$ is a first-order approximation for the earnings function, and we can thus measure θ as revenue per mile driven. The function αh^β captures the notion that whether the uncompensated labour supply function is positively or negatively sloped depends on whether the rate of substitution of leisure for goods increases or decreases at higher work hours.[5] There is nothing in the conventional theory of labour/leisure choice that compels either to be the case, so the issue is entirely an empirical one.

These assumptions lead to a supply function of the form

$$(4) \qquad \ln(h) = (1/\beta) \ln(\theta) - \ln(\alpha/\beta),$$

which is a straightforward log-linear regression. In principle, in this setup fixed effects for individual drivers have the interpretation as variation in α, which affects the level of hours worked, but does not affect the response of hours worked with respect to the wage rate. Note that because of our linear approximation $g(h,y) = \theta h$, we are assuming that individual drivers face perfectly elastic demand schedules for hours worked.[6]

Our estimation strategy is straightforward. We first fit reduced form equations for revenue per mile (θ) and miles driven (h) as functions of monthly dummy variables for the month in which an inspection is observed, a measure of the number of days since the previous inspection, and an indicator for the fare structure in place. We then fit the labour supply function (4) by ordinary least squares and also using the fare indicator variables as instruments. In this context, the fare structure instruments serve two purposes. They permit us to identify a shift along a labour supply function from an exogenous shift in the wage, and they also serve to correct for measurement error that results from the 'division' bias produced from the way in which we construct our measure of revenue per mile.[7]

IV. EMPIRICAL RESULTS

Our identification of the effect of the wage rate on labour supply depends on observing an exogenous wage increase that is not confounded by other factors that would affect labour supply. We use exogenous fare increases for this purpose. It is hard to imagine precisely what other factors would be likely to serve as confounding factors. Factors such as unpredictable increases in the demand for taxi rides (as from a spontaneous demand shock) would not be permanent, while most other shocks would be related to the seasonal or individual driver fixed effects for which we control.[8]

The uncompensated wage-elasticity of labour supply

In Table 3 we report the first-stage results of regressing revenue per mile driven on the fare dummy variables and some other control variables. It is apparent that the fare increases are associated with an average 19% increase in revenue per mile, and that this effect is precisely measured. It is also notable that both the month dummies and the 'days since inspection' variables have very small coefficients, implying that reporting month deviations in revenue per mile are typically within 1–3%.[9]

In Table 4 we report the reduced form regression of miles driven on the fare dummy variables and some other control variables. The results indicate that miles driven decline from 2% to 4% following a fare increase, depending on the specification. The more appropriate specification, which controls for medallion fixed effects, indicates an average 4.2% decline in miles driven. In this exactly identified model, the ratio of these two reduced form estimates is precisely our instrumental variables estimate.

The instrumental variables estimates are reported in Table 5. In what we consider the most appropriate specification, using fixed effects, we estimate an uncompensated labour

© The London School of Economics and Political Science 2010

TABLE 3
(Log) Revenue per Mile as a Function of the Fare Changes (First Stages of Specifications (2) and (4) in Table 5)

	(1) OLS	(2) Fixed effects
Post fare increase*	0.19	0.19
	(0.00)	(0.00)
ln(days since inspection)	− 0.02	− 0.01
	(0.05)	(0.03)
February	− 0.01	0.01
	(0.01)	(0.04)
March	− 0.00	− 0.03
	(0.01)	(0.04)
April	− 0.02	− 0.06
	(0.01)	(0.04)
May	0.00	0.00
	(0.01)	(0.01)
June	− 0.01	0.00
	(0.01)	(0.04)
July	− 0.01	− 0.05
	(0.01)	(0.04)
August	− 0.03	− 0.07
	(0.01)	(0.04)
September	− 0.02	− 0.03
	(0.01)	(0.00)
October	− 0.04	− 0.02
	(0.01)	(0.04)
November	− 0.02	− 0.06
	(0.01)	(0.04)
December	− 0.03	− 0.07
	(0.01)	(0.04)
Constant	− 0.18	− 0.21
	(0.24)	(0.15)
Observations	12,281	12,281
R-squared	0.24	0.53
Number of medallions		2514

Notes

Standard errors in parentheses. Unit of observation: one driver during a four-month period. Fixed effects: medallion level.

*Post fare increase = 0 for inspections that take place during the 365 days before each fare change was implemented. Post fare increase = 1 for inspections that take place during the 365 days beginning four months after each fare change was implemented.

supply elasticity of − 0.23, with a standard error only about one-tenth that size. This is our preferred estimate of these drivers' uncompensated wage-elasticity of labour supply and it is estimated with considerable precision.

There are two other determinants of labour supply that might well have changed at the same time that the fare changed and as a result of its change: (a) a driver's incentive to rent their medallion to others may have increased because of the increased medallion

© The London School of Economics and Political Science 2010

TABLE 4
(Log) Miles Driven as a Function of the Fare Changes

	(1) OLS	(2) Fixed effects
Post fare increase*	− 0.0239	− 0.0423
	(0.00618)	(0.00374)
ln(days since inspection)	0.633	0.792
	(0.102)	(0.0643)
February	− 0.000746	0.0318
	(0.0168)	(0.0906)
March	− 0.0293	− 0.00251
	(0.0154)	(0.0888)
April	− 0.00813	− 0.0492
	(0.0156)	(0.0888)
May	0.0151	0.0219
	(0.0180)	(0.0106)
June	0.0426	0.0608
	(0.0167)	(0.0904)
July	− 0.0154	0.0177
	(0.0156)	(0.0888)
August	− 0.0107	− 0.0393
	(0.0154)	(0.0888)
September	− 0.0231	− 0.0135
	(0.0173)	(0.0100)
October	− 0.0125	0.0363
	(0.0171)	(0.0908)
November	− 0.0300	− 0.00338
	(0.0154)	(0.0888)
December	− 0.00118	− 0.0432
	(0.0154)	(0.0888)
Constant	6.489	5.726
	(0.492)	(0.318)
Observations	12,281	12,281
R-squared	0.007	0.033
Number of medallions		2514

Notes
Standard errors in parentheses. Unit of observation: one driver during a four-month period. Fixed effects: medallion level.
*Post fare increase = 0 for inspections that take place during the 365 days before each fare change was implemented. Post fare increase = 1 for inspections that take place during the 365 days beginning four months after each fare change was implemented.

rental rate; and (b) the value of the medallion on the medallion transaction market may have increased. We examine these issues in order to see what, if any, effect they may have on the interpretations of our primary empirical results.

The change in the medallion rental rate

We do not observe the medallion rental rates over time. However, we know that in 1996 the TLC raised the cap medallion lease, but in 2004 the TLC raised the cap medallion

TABLE 5

(LOG) MILES DRIVEN AS A FUNCTION OF (LOG) REVENUE PER MILE

	(1) OLS	(2) OLS IV	(3) Fixed effects	(4) Fixed effects IV
ln(real revenue per mile)	− 0.42	− 0.13	− 0.40	− 0.23
	(0.01)	(0.03)	(0.01)	(0.02)
ln(days since inspection)	0.63	0.63	0.72	0.79
	(0.06)	(0.10)	(0.04)	(0.06)
February	0.00	− 0.00	0.02	0.04
	(0.01)	(0.02)	(0.02)	(0.09)
March	− 0.03	− 0.03	− 0.00	− 0.01
	(0.01)	(0.02)	(0.02)	(0.09)
April	− 0.01	− 0.01	− 0.04	− 0.06
	(0.01)	(0.02)	(0.02)	(0.09)
May	0.02	0.02	0.02	0.02
	(0.01)	(0.02)	(0.01)	(0.01)
June	0.03	0.04	0.04	0.06
	(0.01)	(0.02)	(0.02)	(0.09)
July	− 0.01	− 0.02	0.02	0.01
	(0.01)	(0.02)	(0.02)	(0.09)
August	− 0.02	− 0.01	− 0.05	− 0.06
	(0.01)	(0.02)	(0.02)	(0.09)
September	− 0.02	− 0.03	− 0.02	− 0.02
	(0.01)	(0.02)	(0.01)	(0.01)
October	− 0.01	− 0.02	− 0.01	0.03
	(0.01)	(0.02)	(0.02)	(0.09)
November	− 0.04	− 0.03	− 0.02	− 0.01
	(0.01)	(0.02)	(0.02)	(0.09)
December	− 0.03	− 0.00	− 0.05	− 0.06
	(0.01)	(0.02)	(0.02)	(0.09)
Constant	6.38	6.46	5.95	5.67
	(0.31)	(0.48)	(0.18)	(0.31)
Observations	33,962	12,281	33,962	12,244
R-squared	0.06	0.03	0.07	
Number of medallions		2645		2514

Notes

Standard errors in parentheses. Unit of observation: one driver during a four-month period. Instrument: 1996 fare increase and 2004 fare increase. Fixed effects: medallion level.

lease rate by only 8% in order that most of the fare increase 'would end up in drivers' pockets'. (See the timeline in the Appendix for more details.) Although we cannot document all the details, there is a potential for large changes in the lease rate around the time of the fare changes that might affect the labour supply of drivers who own medallions, despite the fact that these lease rates do not affect them directly, because of the potential incentives that a change in the lease rate might give an owner–driver.

For example, this change in the incentive to lease to others could potentially cause at least one serious bias: it could selectively remove people from our sample after the fare increase, because they then start renting their evening shift to others.

Since our dataset contains the universe of drivers inspected by the TLC between 1990 and 2005, we may examine the number of medallions that switched from being associated

© The London School of Economics and Political Science 2010

with an owner–driver to being associated with both an owner–driver and another driver, after the fare increases were announced. The data on switchers show that this type of selection affected less than 1% of our sample.[10] Thus it seems unlikely that increased medallion renting has any effect on our results.

The change in the price of the medallion

The New York City taxi medallion is a major asset. In December 2005, the average nominal transaction price in the market for individual medallions was $350,000. A change in the medallion's value occurring at the same time as the fare change could lead to two biases: (a) it could selectively remove someone from our sample because they sell their medallion in response to the jump in its value; and (b) for those who remain in our sample, it might affect their labour supply via an additional income effect. We can examine the first issue by looking at the number of individually owned medallions sold around the time of the fare changes. We regress the number of medallions sold per month on the dummy for post fare increase and on month-of-the-year dummies. In results not reported, we find that the fare increases are associated with an extra 1.4 medallions sold per month, or 17 extra per year, and the increase is not statistically significant. This point estimate thus suggests that perhaps 1% of our sample selected to leave through selling their medallions, which seems unlikely to affect our results.

Finally, to examine possible income effects due to medallion price increases, we examined the time series of monthly average medallion prices reported in Schaller (2006). Medallions trade in an open, public market and the prices are likely to be affected by many factors, including whether the City increases its supply, which it does from time to time (see the timeline in the Appendix), and caps that the TLC places on lease rates. Clearly, both the former and the latter are likely to drive prices down. The time series around the 1996 fare increase does not provide any evidence of medallion price increases, but the time series around the 2004 fare is more suggestive. It is clear that starting around September 2001 there was an upward trend in the price of medallions. It is clear that between September 2001 and April 2004 (when the new fare was announced), the trend in prices was almost linear, whereas as soon as the new fare took effect in May, the trend began to be broken. Fitting the data between September 2001 and April 2004 to a linear time trend shows that a rate of increase of $1834 per month gives an R-squared of 0.95. This trend may thus represent a good counterfactual for what would have happened if the fare change had not been implemented. Using this counterfactual, we calculate that by December 2005, when our dataset ends, the medallions were priced at $53,000 more than they would have been without the fare change.

Is a $50,000 increase in the value of a medallion likely to affect the continuing labour supply of an owner–driver separately from the wage increase with which it is associated? The answer to this question depends on the foresight and age of a driver. To the extent that the owner–driver continues to work and expects to do so for a long time, the income effect produced by the fare increase is entirely captured by the observed fare increase, just as any permanent wage increase affects a worker's lifetime income. However, for workers with shorter horizons, there may be other effects.

According to revenue information from our dataset and cost information from the *New York City Taxicab Fact Book* (Schaller 2006), the drivers in our sample could expect to generate net earnings of about $50,000 per year over the course of their careers, so the medallion price increase is about equivalent to a single year of pay. Assuming an average career length of 30 years, the medallion price increase would constitute about 3% of

© The London School of Economics and Political Science 2010

648   ECONOMICA   [OCTOBER

lifetime income, while the medallion price increase would increase lifetime income by only about 3%. This suggests that any direct effects of the medallion price increase on owner–driver labour supply will be small.

V. CONCLUSIONS

Our results imply that the uncompensated labour supply elasticity for taxi drivers is almost certainly negative and small. This will come as no surprise to those who know the extensive literature devoted to the study of male labour supply. In addition, this finding is consistent with a broad variety of historical evidence that suggests that the massive increases in real wages seen in the USA and Europe since 1879 have been accompanied by significant declines in annual hours worked per worker. It is also consistent with the evidence that work hours are longer in poorer countries than in richer ones.

An important limitation of our results is that they capture only one margin on which labour supply is adjusted, neglecting especially issues of labour force participation and retirement. These participation issues may loom especially large for groups whose attachment to the labour force is not as strong as the primarily adult male workers who make up the bulk of taxi drivers.

Our results have important implications for much of the continuing discussion of tax and transfer programmes in many countries. Many of these discussions continue to operate in nearly complete ignorance of the extensive scientific evidence about labour supply behaviour that has been accumulated over the last four decades. No doubt this is a product, in part, of wishful thinking, but results like those in this paper, replicated in a variety of settings, might serve as a useful antidote for those who are prepared to examine the facts.

APPENDIX: TIMELINE REGARDING TAXI DECISIONS AFTER 1998

All hyperlink sources last accessed 2 June 2010.

13 May 1998
City-wide taxi drivers strike.
(http://socialjustice.ccnmtl.columbia.edu/index.php/Alliance_Achievements)
28 May 1998
City-wide taxi drivers strike.
(http://socialjustice.ccnmtl.columbia.edu/index.php/Alliance_Achievements)
March 2002
The New York City Taxi Workers Alliance organized a forum to hear taxi drivers' stories of their financial deterioration after 11 September. The Federal Emergency Management Agency (FEMA) had assisted taxi garages and brokers but not the drivers, and at this hearing FEMA officials heard the taxi drivers' stories. Soon afterwards, FEMA opened a new Rental and Mortgage Assistance programme; over 2000 drivers participated.
(http://socialjustice.ccnmtl.columbia.edu/index.php/Alliance_Achievements)
29 September 2003
'A group representing thousands of taxi drivers said it would begin to push harder for an increase in fares, after a broad survey of drivers found that many—facing higher gas prices and a weak economy—are increasingly unable to support themselves with their jobs. The survey, to be released today, included 581 drivers who were interviewed at Kennedy International and La Guardia Airports last winter. It was the first time such a large group had been interviewed by the New York Taxi Workers Alliance, which represents 4,800 of the more than 40,000 licensed taxi drivers in the city.'
(http://query.nytimes.com/gst/fullpage.html?res=9F02E1D7103DF93AA1575AC0A9659C8B63)
20 October 2003
'A group representing thousands of taxi drivers in New York City is threatening a strike if the Taxi and Limousine Commission does not enact its first fare increase in seven years.'

© The London School of Economics and Political Science 2010

(http://query.nytimes.com/gst/fullpage.html?res=9407E5DE113EF933A15753C1A9659C8B63)
1 January 2004
'A formal study ordered by the city has essentially cleared the way for the largest taxicab-fleet expansion in nearly 70 years. It concluded that adding 900 cabs over the next three years would not pose environmental concerns and indicated that a moderate fare ease would probably assuage taxi owners.'

'The intention is for 300 cabs to be added in each of the next three years, with the first group expected to be cruising city streets by June.'

(http://wirednewyork.com/forum/showthread.php?t=4273)
12 January 2004
'In recent months, drivers have threatened to strike if the fare is not increased. Officials are currently proposing a 25 percent hike.'

(http://www.gothamgazette.com/print/833)
28 January 2004
The TLC officially proposes taxi fare adjustment and service improvements.

(http://www.nyc.gov/html/tlc/html/news/press04_01.shtml)
'The proposal comes in the midst of environmental reviews for issuance of 900 additional taxicab licenses over three years, with the first batch of 300 planned for issuance by the end of the current fiscal year on June 30.'

(http://www.gothamgazette.com/article/transportation/20040224/16/889)
30 March 2004
The TLC officially approves a fare increase of more than 26 percent, to take effect on Monday 3 May.

(http://query.nytimes.com/gst/fullpage.html?res=9502E7DB1739F932A05750C0A9629C8B63&sec=&spon=&pagewanted=print)
'Most of the increase will end up in drivers' pockets, because the commission also ruled that lease caps—the maximum amount that fleet owners can charge drivers—can be raised by only 8 percent.'

(http://wirednewyork.com/forum/showthread.php?t=4273)
'The New York City Taxi and Limousine Commission (TLC) today unanimously approved a proposed fare adjustment, as well as a package of service improvements designed to enhance the taxi riding experience. The new fare formula will be in effect as of 12:01 a.m. Monday, May 3, 2004.'

(http://www.nyc.gov/html/tlc/html/news/press04_03_a.shtml)
16 April 2004
'On April 16, bids for 174 medallions from corporations (medallion and/or fleet owners) were accepted.'

23 April 2004
'On April 23, 126 more new medallions were sold at a second bid opening for individuals . . .'

'On April 16 and 23, the New York City Taxi and Limousine Commission (TLC) opened some 664 bids for a total of 300 new yellow taxi medallions being auctioned by the city.'

(http://www.unitedspinal.org/publications/action/2004/06/25/new-taxi-medallions-sold-no-access-achieved)
3 May 2004
Fare increase comes into effect.

(http://www.allbusiness.com/transportation-communications/transportation-services/4156824-1.html)
4 May 2004
Fare increase noticeable in the data.

ACKNOWLEDGMENTS

We are indebted to Henry Farber, Derek Neal, John Pencavel and Robert Solow, and to participants at the Conference in Honour of Richard Layard and Steve Nickell held at the Center for Economic Performance in June 2009 for very helpful comments on this paper. We are also indebted to Nicholas Lawson for outstanding research assistance.

© The London School of Economics and Political Science 2010

NOTES

1. See the comprehensive and influential surveys by Pencavel (1986), Heckman and Killingsworth (1986), and Blundell and MaCurdy (1999) for the details. Formal evidence that workers face constraints on hours worked within jobs dates from at least Ham (1982) and Altonji and Paxson (1988).
2. A comprehensive source, on which we rely for much of the following material, is Bruce Schaller (2006).
3. The potential linkage between driver labour supply and miles driven would ideally be studied with some measure of actual hours worked or clocked, which is not available at this time. However, in our analyses we do control for driver fixed effects and for month variability, and it seems likely that much of the systematic variation in driver down time that otherwise exists will be unrelated to the timing of fare changes.
4. Only 2535 of these medallions have sufficient meter information for revenue and related calculations.
5. This functional form was first apparently used by Burtless and Hausman (1978), and the implied utility function and other aspects of it are discussed extensively by Stern (1986).
6. It is important to understand that even though the demand curve for aggregate taxi rides is downward sloping, this is not the demand curve that individual drivers face. Our assumption about the driver's revenue function implies that an individual driver may drive as much as they like at the equilibrium price in the aggregate market.
7. This measurement error tends to produce an automatic negative correlation between miles driven and revenue per mile, because the former is contained in the denominator of the latter. Measurement errors in miles driven thus result in a spurious negative correlation between miles driven and revenue per mile. See especially Farber (2005) for a discussion of this issue.
8. One exception might be gasoline prices, which form an important cost for a driver. However, gasoline prices were very stable in the period surrounding the 1996 fare increase. Gasoline prices were on an increasing path during the period surrounding the 2004 fare increase, which would imply that we have somewhat underestimated the increase in real revenues per mile driven and therefore underestimated (in absolute value) the labour supply elasticity.
9. Recall from the discussion above that the 'month' dummy variables record the month that the taxi inspection took place. These inspections cover a 4-month period. Thus the coefficients on the month dummies are linear combinations of effects that would be estimated with dummy variables that measured the revenue per mile in an actual calendar month.
10. There are 17 medallions in our sample that were owner–driver medallions as of March 2004 but became medallions associated with both an owner–driver and another driver after March 2004 (i.e. after the announcement of the fare increase). Assuming that all of these drivers sought out partners because of the increased lease rates, this would mean that the selection rate was 17 out of the total of 2705 medallions in our sample. According to our data, no medallions that were associated only with an owner–driver before the 1996 fare increase later appear as associated with an owner–driver and another driver after the 1996 fare increase. Dividing 17 by 2705 gives a selection rate of under 1%.

REFERENCES

ALTONJI, J. G. and PAXSON, C. H. (1988). Labor supply preferences, hours constraints, and hours-wage trade-offs. *Journal of Labor Economics*, **6**(2), 254–76.

BLUNDELL, R. and MACURDY, T. (1999). Labor supply: a review of alternative approaches. In O. Ashenfelter and D. Card (eds), *Handbook of Labor Economics*, Vol. 3. Amsterdam: Elsevier, pp. 1559–695.

BURTLESS, G. and HAUSMAN, J. A. (1978). The effect of taxation on labor supply: evaluating the Gary negative income tax experiment. *Journal of Political Economy*, **86**(6), 1103–30.

FARBER, H. (2005). Is tomorrow another day? The labor supply of New York City cab drivers. *Journal of Political Economy*, **113**(February), 46–82.

HAM, J. (1982). Estimation of a labour supply model with censoring due to unemployment and underemployment. *Review of Economic Studies*, **49**(3), 335–54.

HECKMAN, M. R. and KILLINGSWORTH, J. J. (1986). Female labor supply: a survey. In O. Ashenfelter and R. Layard (eds), *Handbook of Labor Economics*, Vol. 1. Amsterdam: Elsevier, pp. 103–204.

PENCAVEL, J. (1986). Labor supply of men: a survey. In O. Ashenfelter and R. Layard (eds), *Handbook of Labor Economics*, Vol. 1. Amsterdam: Elsevier, pp. 3–102.

SCHALLER, B. (2006). *The New York City Taxicab Fact Book*. Brooklyn, NY: Schaller Consulting.

STERN, N. (1986). On the specification of labour supply functions. In R. Blundell and I. Walker (eds), *Unemployment, Search and Labour Supply*. Cambridge: Cambridge University Press, pp. 143–89.

© The London School of Economics and Political Science 2010

The ups and downs of minimum wage

by Diane Galarneau and Eric Fecteau

Overview of the study

This article provides information on the evolution of the minimum wage in Canada since 1975, the average hourly earnings, and the ratio between these two indicators. It also sheds light on the increase in the proportion of employees paid at the minimum wage between 1997 and 2013, as well as the characteristics of workers most likely to be paid at this minimum rate.

- In 2013, the minimum wage was around $10 in all provinces. In constant dollars, this rate was similar to the rate observed in the late 1970s.

- The minimum wage is often expressed as a proportion of average hourly earnings, but this ratio can vary depending on the data source used. In 2013, the overall minimum wage rate was between 42% and 49% of the average hourly earnings, depending on the source.

- Between 1997 and 2013, the proportion of employees paid at minimum wage increased from 5.0% to 6.7%. The bulk of this increase occurred between 2003 and 2010.

- When the minimum wage is revised upward, the proportion of employees paid at minimum wage may increase. This is because some employees whose wage was previously above the old level are paid the new rate, and join those who were already earning the minimum wage.

- The profile of minimum wage workers did not change between 1997 and 2013, as young workers, less-educated workers and workers in the service sectors were still more likely to be paid the minimum wage.

Introduction

Minimum wage studies generate substantial interest, given the links often made between the minimum wage, employment, and poverty. While there is no consensus on how the minimum wage affects poverty and inequality,[1] the association with employment is well-documented. In Canada, the effects of an increase in the minimum wage on total employment would typically be small or non-existent.[2] Rather, an increase in the minimum wage would seem to be associated with a decrease in employment among teenagers,[3] who are most likely to be paid at this hourly rate.

The extent of the effect on employment depends on a number of factors,[4] including the ratio of the minimum wage to the average hourly earnings (AHE). The higher this ratio—that is, the closer the minimum wage to average hourly earnings (all things being equal)—the more workers are affected by minimum wage legislation and the greater the effects on employment.[5] These effects do not necessarily take the form of layoffs, but may instead take the form of reduced hiring, which diminishes the job prospects of teenagers.[6]

The ups and downs of minimum wage

This article begins by examining how the real minimum wage, average hourly earnings and the ratio between these two indicators have evolved since 1975, based on data from the Survey of Employment, Payrolls and Hours (SEPH) and the Labour Force Survey (LFS).

Then, the article investigates the slight increase in the proportion of employees paid at minimum wage, which went from 5.0% in 1997 to 6.7% in 2013. It also looks at the characteristics of employees paid at minimum wage to determine whether the recent increase in the proportion of such workers is due to a change in their profile. In other words, are some groups of employees more likely to be paid at minimum wage than in the late 1990s?

The real minimum wage is similar to the level observed in the late 1970s

In Canada, minimum wage legislation is of provincial jurisdiction, and therefore may vary from one province to another. A value for the minimum wage for Canada can be obtained by calculating the average of provincial minimum wages, weighted by the employment levels of each of the 10 provinces since 1975. These values can then be adjusted for inflation using the consumer price index (CPI) for each province to obtain a "Canadian" real minimum wage (in 2013 dollars).

Since 1975, the average Canadian real minimum wage varied between $7 and $11, peaking in 1975 and 1976 (Chart 1). Subsequently, the average minimum wage declined to under $8 in the mid-1980s, and did not change much until 2005. It then began rising again, reaching approximately $10 in 2010 and stayed around this level up to 2013.

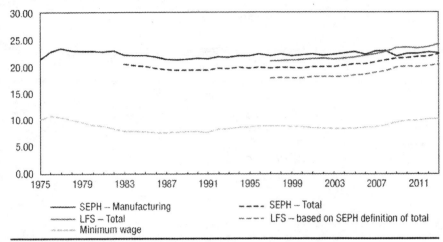

Chart 1
The minimum wage[1] in 2013 was similar to the level in the late 1970s in real terms

average hourly earnings and minimum wage (2013 dollars)[2]

— SEPH – Manufacturing   ---- SEPH – Total
— LFS – Total   ---- LFS – based on SEPH definition of total
  Minimum wage

1. The minimum wage for Canada is the average of the minimum wages of the provinces, weighted by the number of employees in each province.
2. The average hourly earnings and the minimum wage are expressed in 2013 constant dollars, based on the consumer price indexes of each province.

Notes: The average hourly earnings from the SEPH (manufacturing sector and total) are those of employees paid by the hour, whereas the LFS series for all employees includes both employees who are paid by the hour and employees with a fixed salary. The LFS series based on the SEPH definition of the total includes employees paid by the hour from all sectors, except in agriculture and other services.

Sources: Statistics Canada, Survey of Employment, Payrolls and Hours (SEPH); Labour Force Survey (LFS); Employment and Social Development Canada (minimum hourly rates by year and by province).

In the case of average hourly earnings (AHE), the level may vary, depending on the source. In this article, two sources are used: the Survey of Employment, Payrolls and Hours (SEPH), which collects information from businesses on the wages paid to their employees; and the Labour Force Survey (LFS), which collects data from households on the 'usual' earnings of paid workers (see *Data sources, methods and definitions*). Four versions of the AHE were calculated:

1) The AHE of employees paid by the hour in the manufacturing sector in the SEPH from 1975 to 2013

2) The AHE of employees paid by the hour for all industrial sectors in the SEPH from 1983 to 2013

3) The AHE of employees paid by the hour for all industrial sectors in the LFS from 1997 to 2013[7]

4) The AHE of all paid employees in the LFS (regardless of the method of compensation) from 1997 to 2013.

The SEPH series on the manufacturing sector is the only one going back to 1975. According to that series, the AHE of employees paid by the hour in the manufacturing sector remained fairly stable at around $22 (in 2013 constant dollars) throughout the period. However, this sector's share of total employment declined over time, from 19% in 1975 to 10% in 2013. Furthermore, the gap between the AHE of the manufacturing sector and the AHE of all sectors combined also declined.[8] As a result, the trends exhibited by the manufacturing sector became less representative of the total paid workforce in recent years.

The series of employees paid by the hour in all industrial sectors in the SEPH, which begins in 1983,[9] is more representative of the Canadian paid workforce. According to this series, the AHE remained stable at around $20 until the mid-2000s but gradually increased in recent years, to more than $22 in 2013.

This recent upward trend is also confirmed by the two LFS series, which both begin in 1997. In the first LFS series on employees paid by the hour, the AHE went from $18 in 1997 to $20 in 2013. In the LFS series on all employees, the AHE went from $21 to $24 during the period. The higher AHE levels in the latter series are due to the fact that the AHE covers not only employees paid by the hour but also employees with a fixed salary, who have a higher AHE.

A ratio approaching the values of the mid-1970s

An important indicator of how increases in the minimum wage affect employment is the ratio of the minimum wage to the average hourly earnings (AHE). Since the AHE remained fairly stable throughout the study period, variations in the ratio are largely attributable to changes in the real minimum wage.

Four ratios were calculated based on the four versions of the AHE described above. Although the ratio varies over time and depending on the series used, it is possible to distinguish four major periods: a period of decline between 1975 and 1986, a period of increase between 1986 and 1997, a new decline extending to 2005, and, lastly, another rise between 2005 and 2013 (Chart 2).

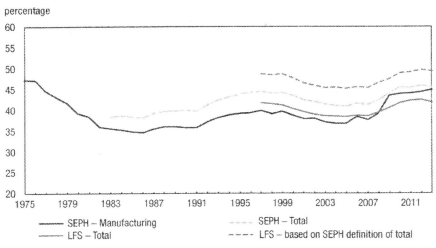

Chart 2
The ratio of the minimum wage[1] to the average hourly earnings[2] is on the rise since the mid-2000s

1. The minimum wage for Canada is the average of the minimum wages of the provinces, weighted by the number of employees in each province.
2. The average hourly earnings and the minimum wage are expressed in 2013 constant dollars, based on the consumer price indexes of each province.

Notes: The average hourly earnings from the SEPH (manufacturing sector and total) are those of employees paid by the hour, whereas the LFS series for all employees includes both employees who are paid by the hour and employees with a fixed salary. The LFS series based on the SEPH definition of the total includes employees paid by the hour from all sectors, except in agriculture and other services.

Sources: Statistics Canada, Survey of Employment, Payrolls and Hours (SEPH); Labour Force Survey (LFS); Employment and Social Development Canada (minimum hourly rates by year and by province).

During the first period, from 1975 to 1986, the series based on SEPH data for the manufacturing sector shows a decline, with the ratio going from a high of 47% in 1976 to a low of 35% in 1986. This decrease was the result of a greater decline in the minimum wage (from $11 to less than $8) than in the AHE (from $23 to $22).

During the second period, from 1986 to 1997, the minimum wage increased by approximately $1 per hour while the AHE remained relatively stable (at nearly $22 in the manufacturing sector and nearly $20 in all sectors combined), which caused the ratio to rise by 5 to 6 percentage points, depending on the series used.

During the third period, from 1997 to 2005, the ratio fell again, dropping 3 to 4 percentage points, since the real minimum wage declined by roughly 40 cents while the AHE rose from 50 to 80 cents, depending on the series.

Finally, starting in 2005, the ratio was generally trending upward, regardless of the series used. The increase mainly occurred from 2005 to 2010, with the ratio subsequently remaining stable (through to 2013). According to the SEPH series on all industrial sectors, the ratio went from 41% in 2005 to 46% in 2013. In the case of the SEPH series on the manufacturing sector, the ratio rose even more (from 37% to 45%). As for the ratio based on the LFS's AHE, the increase went from 39% to 42% for all employees and from 45% to 49% for employees paid by the hour.

Recent rise of the ratio in most provinces

In 1975, the real minimum wage (in 2013 dollars) stood at nearly $10 an hour in all provinces. Even though it evolved differently in each province during the period, in 2013 it was again hovering around $10 in most provinces.

The ratio of the minimum wage to the AHE of each province fluctuated in recent decades, as has been the case in Canada as a whole. However, in the past 10 years, the ratio increased in most provinces (Charts 3.1 to 3.3). This is because the minimum wage has grown more rapidly than the AHE in recent years.[10]

In the Atlantic provinces, the increase started in 2005, with the ratio gaining between 9 and 11 percentage points in each of these provinces. In Newfoundland and Labrador, the ratio even went from 35% in 2005 to 50% in 2010, before falling back to 44% in 2013. In Ontario, the ratio gained more than 7 percentage points starting in 2003 (from 40% to 47%), while in British Columbia it jumped 7 percentage points from 2010 to 2013 (going from 39% to 46%). The ratio also rose in Alberta (starting in 2004) and Manitoba (starting in 2005) by 6 and 7 percentage points respectively.

In contrast, the ratio fluctuated less in Saskatchewan and in Quebec over the period. In Saskatchewan, the ratio varied between 40% and 44% during the whole period, while the ratio in Quebec varied between 44% and 48% during the 2000s.[11]

Chart 3.1
In the Atlantic region, the ratio of the minimum wage to the average hourly earnings has increased since the mid-2000s

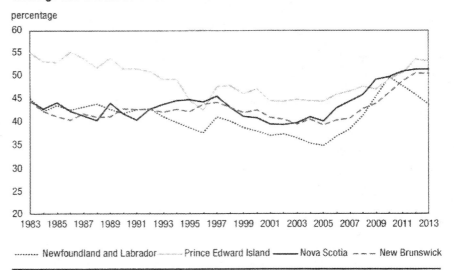

Notes: The average hourly earnings and the minimum wage are expressed in 2013 constant dollars, based on the consumer price indexes of each province. For each province, the average hourly earnings used for this ratio are based on the SEPH data on employees paid by the hour in the province.
Sources: Statistics Canada, Survey of Employment, Payrolls and Hours (SEPH); Employment and Social Development Canada (for minimum hourly rates by year and by province). The ratios were calculated by dividing the minimum wage for each month and year by the average hourly earnings of the corresponding province.

Chart 3.2
Increase in the ratio between 2003 and 2010 in Ontario and stability in Quebec since 2001

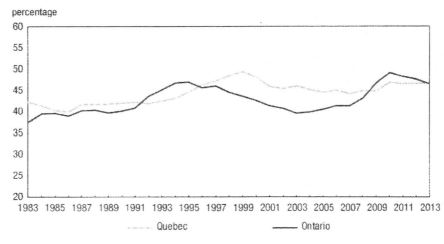

Notes: The average hourly earnings and the minimum wage are expressed in 2013 constant dollars, based on the consumer price indexes of each province. For each province, the average hourly earnings used for this ratio are based on the SEPH data on employees paid by the hour in the province.
Sources: Statistics Canada, Survey of Employment, Payrolls and Hours (SEPH); Employment and Social Development Canada (for minimum hourly rates by year and by province). The ratios were calculated by dividing the minimum wage for each month and year by the average hourly earnings of the corresponding province.

The ups and downs of minimum wage

Recent rise in the proportion of employees paid at minimum wage

Since the LFS began collecting information on the remuneration of paid employees, it has been possible to track the number of employees paid at minimum wage and to express their number as a proportion of the total number of paid employees.[12] Since 1997, there has been a modest increase, from 5.0% to 6.7%, in the proportion of those who are at minimum wage. This increase has sometimes been interpreted as an increase in the proportion of low paid jobs.

However, an increase in the minimum wage can "automatically" increase the proportion of paid employees at minimum wage. This is because when the minimum wage is revised upward, some of the employees whose wage was formerly above the old minimum wage level are now paid at the new rate, and join those who were already earning the minimum wage.

This effect was quite clear among young employees aged 15 to 19 between 2003 and 2010, when the minimum wage increased in a number of provinces. During this period, the rate of young employees working at minimum wage went from 30% to 45% (Chart 4). This increase coincided with a decrease in the proportion of employees in this age group who were paid at a rate between the minimum wage and 10% above the minimum wage; their proportion went from 31% to 21% (not accounting for the possibility of job losses).

Thus, there is a positive correlation between the minimum wage to AHE ratio and the proportion of employees paid at minimum wage.

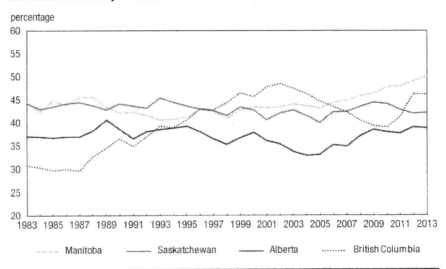

Chart 3.3
Increase in the last few years in Manitoba, Alberta and British Columbia and relative stability in Saskatchewan

Notes: The average hourly earnings and the minimum wage are expressed in 2013 constant dollars, based on the consumer price indexes of each province. For each province, the average hourly earnings used for this ratio are based on the SEPH data on employees paid by the hour in the province.
Sources: Statistics Canada, Survey of Employment, Payrolls and Hours (SEPH); Employment and Social Development Canada (for minimum hourly rates by year and by province). The ratios were calculated by dividing the minimum wage for each month and year by the average hourly earnings of the corresponding province.

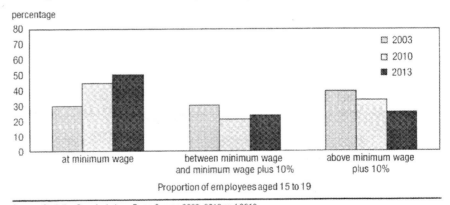

Chart 4
Among paid workers aged 15 to 19, the increase in the proportion of minimum wage employees corresponded with a decrease in the proportion of those earning between the minimum wage and 10% more than the minimum wage

Source: Statistics Canada, Labour Force Survey, 2003, 2010 and 2013.

The higher the ratio and the closer the minimum wage to the AHE, the greater the increase in the proportion of employees paid at minimum wage. As a result, these two indicators typically move in the same direction (Chart 5).[13]

The profile of employees paid at minimum wage has not changed

Has the increase in the minimum wage been proportionally greater for some population groups? The most appropriate source to answer this question is the LFS, since it has wage data going back to 1997 in addition to a large range of sociodemographic characteristics.

In 2013 (as in 1997), youth, women and persons with a low level of education were the groups most likely to be paid at minimum wage (Table 1). In 2013, 50% of employees aged 15 to 19 and 13% of those aged 20 to 24 were paid at minimum wage. Among women, the rate was 8% (compared with 6% among men); among the least-educated, specifically those with less than a high school diploma, the proportion was 20%, compared with less than 3% among university graduates.

Low educational attainment is more often associated with minimum wage among women. In 2013, the rate of working at minimum wage for women aged 25 to 64 with less than a high school diploma varied between 11% and 15%, compared with 4% and 5% among their male counterparts (Chart 6).

Some employment characteristics were also associated with a higher rate. This was the case among part-time employees, 22% of whom earned the minimum wage, as well as employees in the retail trade (17%) and food and accommodation sectors (27%).

Minimum-wage policies affected relatively few employees in Alberta and Saskatchewan. The lowest rate of work at minimum wage in 2013 was in Alberta, at scarcely 2%.[14] Saskatchewan followed with a rate

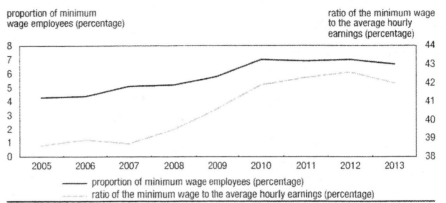

Chart 5
When the ratio of the minimum wage to the average hourly earnings increases, the proportion of minimum wage employees also tends to increase

Sources: Statistics Canada, Labour Force Survey; Employment and Social Development Canada (minimum hourly rates by year and by province), 2005 to 2013.

Table 1
Proportion of minimum wage employees and distribution of employees paid at minimum wage, 1997 and 2013

	Proportion at minimum wage 2013	1997	Distribution of employees at minimum wage 2013	1997
	percentage		thousand	
Total	**6.7**	**5.0**	**1,007.1**	**568.5**
		percentage		
Sex				
Men	5.5	3.9	41.1	40.8
Women	8.0	6.2	58.9	59.2
Age group				
15 to 19	50.2	31.5	39.8	36.0
20 to 24	13.4	9.7	21.0	20.9
25 to 34	3.5	3.0	12.0	16.0
35 to 64	2.8	2.3	24.8	25.8
65 and over	7.0	8.3	2.5	1.3
Education (15 years of age and over)				
Less than a high school diploma	20.4	11.3	29.3	40.1
High school diploma and some postsecondary education	10.2	5.9	41.8	36.3
Postsecondary diploma	3.4	2.7	18.2	17.7
University degree	2.6	1.6	10.6	5.9
Work arrangement				
Full time	3.4	2.8	41.0	45.0
Part time	21.8	14.9	59.0	55.0
Industry				
Goods	2.6	2.1	8.3	10.7
Services	7.8	6.0	91.7	89.3
Retail trade	17.4	10.2	32.9	25.3
Food and accommodation	26.9	21.0	27.8	28.7
Province				
Newfoundland and Labrador	5.9	9.2	1.2	2.7
Prince Edward Island	9.3	4.7	0.6	0.4
Nova Scotia	5.9	7.9	2.3	4.5
New Brunswick	7.9	6.8	2.4	3.2
Quebec	6.2	3.6	21.5	17.2
Ontario	8.9	5.6	51.5	43.4
Manitoba	6.0	3.9	3.2	2.9
Saskatchewan	4.5	5.7	2.0	3.5
Alberta	1.8	3.0	3.3	6.1
British Columbia	6.4	6.1	12.0	16.1

Source: Statistics Canada, Labour Force Survey, 1997 and 2013.

of less than 5%. In contrast, Prince Edward Island and Ontario had the highest proportions (nearly 9%).

Between 1997 and 2013, the proportion of employees paid at minimum wage increased across the board (except for those aged 65 and over and employees in some provinces such as Alberta, Saskatchewan, Newfoundland and Labrador, and Nova Scotia), meaning no subgroups are more likely today than in 1997 to be represented among employees paid at minimum wage.[15]

As a result, the profile of employees paid at minimum wage did not change much during the period, since the great majority of them are still youth, part-time employees and employees in service industries. Hence, 61% of minimum wage employees were aged 15 to 24 in 2013 (57% in 1997). Also, 59% of them held a part-time job in 2013 (55% in 1997). Finally, in 2013, 61% of all minimum wage employees were in the retail trade or food and accommodation sectors (54% in 1997).

Conclusion

This article has examined the change, in constant dollars, of the minimum wage, average hourly earnings (AHE) and the ratio between these two indicators in Canada and the provinces since 1975. Although the real minimum wage varied over the period, the 2013 minimum wage was almost identical to levels seen in the mid 1970s. To study the ratio between the minimum wage and average earnings, several versions of the AHE were used, with some covering a relatively long observation period, and others covering a shorter period. Although the ratio results vary depending on the source used for the AHE, four periods can be identified: a decrease in the ratio, covering the years 1975 to 1986; a rebound, between 1986 and 1997; then another decline, between 1997 and 2005; and finally another increase, between 2005 and 2013. Since the AHE remained relatively stable throughout the study period, changes in the ratio are largely attributable to changes in the real minimum wage.

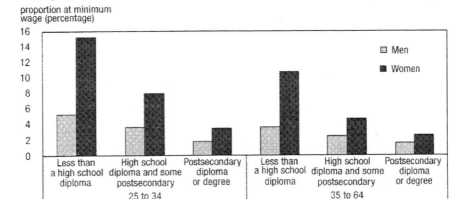

Chart 6
A lower level of education is most often associated with minimum wage among women

Source: Statistics Canada, Labour Force Survey, 2013.

Between 1997 and 2013, the proportion of employees paid at minimum wage went up, from 5.0% to 6.7%. This increase mainly occurred between 2003 and 2010, when a number of provinces raised their hourly minimum rate. Increases in the minimum wage often correspond with an increase in the proportion of employees paid at minimum wage. This was especially true for paid workers aged 15 to 19: between 2003 and 2010, the proportion paid at minimum wage rate increased by 15 percentage points, while the share of those paid at a rate between the minimum wage and 10% above the minimum wage decreased by 10 percentage points during the same period.

While the share of employees earning the minimum wage increased between 1997 and 2013 for most population groups, the groups most likely to be paid at this wage remained the same. In 2013, like in 1997, youth, less-educated individuals and part-time employees were more likely to be paid at minimum wage. The retail trade sector and the food and accommodation sector still had the largest proportion of workers paid at minimum wage.

Diane Galarneau is a senior analyst in the Labour Statistics Division of Statistics Canada and Eric Fecteau is a student participating to the University of Ottawa co-operative education program.

The ups and downs of minimum wage

Data sources, methods and definitions

Data sources

This article is based on the Survey of Employment, Payrolls and Hours (SEPH) and the Labour Force Survey (LFS). Residents from the Northwest Territories, Yukon and Nunavut have been excluded because these regions are not included in these surveys for the entire study period.

On a monthly basis, the SEPH provides information about earnings, number of jobs (i.e. occupied positions), vacant positions and hours worked, by detailed industry, at the national, provincial and territorial levels. Monthly survey estimates are produced by a combination of a census of payroll deductions provided by the Canada Revenue Agency and the Business Payrolls Survey (BPS), which collects data from a sample of 15,000 businesses.

The Labour Force Survey (LFS) is a monthly household survey of about 54,000 households across Canada. Demographic and labour force information is obtained for all household members 15 years of age and over. Excluded are persons living in institutions, on Indian reserves or in the territories.

Definitions

Average hourly earnings

For several decades, the SEPH has been calculating an average hourly earnings rate for employees whose mode of compensation is "paid by the hour." In 2013, these workers accounted for 58% of all workers in establishments classified in the SEPH, up from 52% in 2004 and 47% in 1983. The other categories are "employees with a fixed salary" (35% of workers in 2013) and employees paid otherwise, such as on a piecework basis (7% in 2013). Since 1983, businesses of all sizes have been included in the sample, whereas, before 1983, businesses with fewer than 20 employees were excluded.

With regard to the LFS, average hourly wage levels can be calculated back to 1997, either for all workers or for employees paid by the hour. In the LFS, only "usual" earnings are included, whereas in the SEPH, all types of earnings are included, including bonuses.

Four versions of the average hourly earnings are used in this article: two from the SEPH and two from the LFS:

1. The first series, based on the SEPH, covers workers paid by the hour (excluding overtime) in the manufacturing sector in each province for the period from 1975 to 2013. The data have been retrieved from CANSIM tables 281-0022, 281-0004 and 281-0029.

2. The second series, also based on the SEPH, covers all workers paid by the hour (excluding overtime). The data have been retrieved from CANSIM tables 281-0004 and 281-0029. This series begins in 1983, after businesses with fewer than 20 employees were added to the survey.

3. The third series was calculated using the LFS, but on the basis of workers paid by the hour in industrial sectors covered by the SEPH (i.e. all industries except agriculture and other services). This series begins in 1997, when the LFS began collecting information on compensation.

4. The fourth series was calculated from the LFS and covers all paid workers in all industrial sectors, whether they are paid by the hour or otherwise. In this series that also begins in 1997, the AHE is higher since the hourly earnings of employees with a fixed salary are higher than those of workers paid by the hour on average.

Minimum wage

Minimum hourly rates are obtained from Employment and Social Development Canada (ESDC) and can be viewed at http://srv116.services.gc.ca/dimt-wid/sm-mw/rpt2.aspx?lang=eng&dec=1.

The minimum wage for Canada as a whole is the average of the monthly minimum wages of the provinces, weighted by the number of workers in each province (see CANSIM tables 281-0015, 281-0001 and 281-0023). The number of employees for the federal government was unavailable from 1975 to 1982, but it was estimated at 40% of the number of all government employees for this period (percentage based on the values recorded for 1975). Starting in July 1996, the minimum wage for federal employees was that which prevailed in their province of employment. Therefore, no distinction has been made starting from that date.

Values in 2013 constant dollars

The values for the minimum wage and the average hourly earnings in real dollars were obtained using the all-items consumer price index specific to each province (see CANSIM table 326-0021).

Minimum wage legislation

The minimum wage—the lowest wage rate that an employer can pay its employees—is dictated by labour laws. Since these laws are under provincial jurisdiction, all Canadian provinces set a minimum hourly rate, which is adjusted periodically.

Self-employed workers and unpaid family workers are not covered by minimum wage legislation and are not included in this analysis. Other exclusions and special implementation provisions vary by year and province. For example, minimum wage legislation does not apply to domestic and family aid workers living with the employer (Alberta, New Brunswick, Prince Edward Island, Manitoba, British Columbia and Quebec); agricultural workers (Ontario); and home workers. Special minimum-wage rates may apply to some workers with non-hourly pay and tips.

In this article, minimum wage workers are those who receive the "minimum wage for experienced adult workers" that is set by their province. Also included are workers who receive a wage below this threshold. Hourly earnings below the established minimum do not necessarily indicate an infringement of the law—they may be received by workers not subject to the law or subject to rates below the minimum wage, such as some workers in food services (e.g. servers).

The proportion of workers paid minimum wage is obtained by calculating the number of employees working at minimum wage for each province and for each month since 1997. The annual estimate for each province is based on the average of the 12 monthly observations, while the total for Canada is the average of the provincial estimates.

The ups and downs of minimum wage

Notes

1. According to some analysts, regulating the minimum wage is not very effective in combating poverty since people paid at minimum wage do not necessarily belong to a low-income household (Neumark and Wascher 2008; Gunderson 2008). According to the SLID, 10% of workers paid at minimum wage belonged to families whose family income was below the poverty threshold in 2011. However, Fortin and Lemieux (1997) found that regulating the minimum wage can contribute to income redistribution because minimum-wage workers are more likely than other workers to belong to low-income families. Fortin and Lemieux (2014) also illustrated that increases in the minimum wage explain much of the relatively faster increase in wages in the lower income quintile in Canada since 2005 (compared with the median quintile).

2. See Baker et al. (1999); Gunderson (2008), Fortin (2010); Lemieux (2011); Brochu and Green (2012).

3. The negative effect on employment is higher in Canada than in the United States. See Gunderson (2008) and Fortin (2010) for more information on this subject.

4. These factors include globalization, changes in technology and shifts in the unionization rate.

5. The effect on employment varies between 3% and 6%, depending on the study. According to Fortin (2010), when the ratio is close to 50%, the effects on the employment of teenagers are relatively significant.

6. According to Brochu and Green (2012), when the minimum wage is high, labour market transitions (hirings and layoffs) tend to decrease. For teenagers, the reductions in hirings largely exceed the number of layoffs, which explains why there is a significant and negative effect on employment in this age group. For older workers, the reduction in layoffs largely offsets the reduction in hirings, with a nil or insignificant effect on employment.

7. Excluding agriculture and other services, which are not covered by the SEPH.

8. From the mid-1980s to 2005, the AHE of the manufacturing sector was 8% to 13% higher than that of all sectors combined but, by 2013, this gap had shrunk to approximately 1%.

9. Since 1983, the SEPH's AHE data have covered businesses of all sizes, whereas before 1983 they covered only those with 20 employees and more. The inclusion of small businesses caused the AHE to decline after 1982. However, the series on the manufacturing sector exhibits a fairly stable trend, since this sector is largely made up of businesses with 20 employees and more. For this reason, it was used to calculate the ratio in the years prior to the redesign of the SEPH.

10. The SEPH series on hourly paid employees for all industrial sectors was used to analyze the ratios by province, because it is representative of a greater share of employees (approximately 65% of paid employees in 2013) than the series focusing solely on the manufacturing sector (which accounted for slightly more than 11% of employees paid by the hour in 2013) and also because it covers three decades. In 2013, the highest AHE was recorded in Alberta ($25) and the lowest in Prince Edward Island ($19). In 1983, this gap was higher, with the AHE ranging from $14 in Prince Edward Island to $23 in British Columbia. All data on real minimum wage, the real AHE and the ratio between these two indicators for Canada and the provinces from 1983 to 2013 are available in Table A.1 (appended).

11. Even though the levels were different, similar trends were recorded starting in 1997 for the two LFS series, namely an increase in the ratio because the minimum wage grew more rapidly than the AHE in most provinces.

12. The LFS assigns an hourly wage to employees not paid by the hour, based on the answers that respondents provide on hours worked. Those who earn less than or equivalent to the minimum wage in the province where they reside are thus considered as being paid at minimum wage.

13. This correlation is verified using a linear regression model covering the period from 1997 to 2013, in which the dependent variable is the proportion at the minimum wage by province and the independent variables are the ratio and dummy variables for each province. The coefficient estimated by the ratio was 0.40, which means that a 1 percentage point increase in the ratio was associated with a 0.4 percentage point increase in the rate of employment at minimum wage.

The ups and downs of minimum wage

14. Since the minimum wage is fairly similar from one province to another (around $10), most of the interprovincial differences were not due to differences in minimum-wage levels.

15. The results of an Oaxaca decomposition model confirm that the increase in the proportion of minimum wage employees is not due to a change in worker composition. In other words, it is not due to an increase in the proportion of total employment held by workers more likely to be paid the minimum wage.

References

Baker, Michael, Dwayne Benjamin and Shuchita Stanger. 1999. "The highs and lows of the minimum wage effect: A time-series cross-section study of the Canadian law." Journal of Labour Economics. Vol. 17, no. 2. April. p. 318-350.

Brochu Pierre and David A. Green. 2012. *The Impact of Minimum Wages on Labour Market Transitions.* October. University of British Columbia, Vancouver School of Economics.

Fortin, Nicole M. and Thomas Lemieux. 2014 *Changes in Wage Inequality in Canada: An Interprovincial Perspective.* January. University of British Columbia, Department of Economics. 54 p.

Fortin, Nicole M. and Thomas Lemieux. 1997. "Institutional changes and rising wage inequality: Is there a linkage?" Journal of Economic Perspectives. Vol. 11, no. 2. Spring p. 75-96.

Fortin, Pierre. 2010. "Salaire minimum, pauvreté et emploi : à la recherche du compromis idéal." Regards sur le travail. Vol. 7, no. 1. Autumn.

Gunderson, Morley. 2008. *Minimum Wages: Operating with a Blunt Instrument.* Aims Labour Market Series. Commentary no. 1. December. Atlantic Institute for Market Studies.

Lemieux, Thomas. 2011. *Minimum Wages and the Joint Distribution of Employment and Wages.* Research Paper. October. University of British Columbia and National Bureau of Economic Research.

Neumark, David and William L. Wascher. 2008. *Minimum Wages.* Cambridge, MA. The MIT Press. 392 p.

The ups and downs of minimum wage

Appendix

Table A.1
Real minimum wage, average hourly earnings and ratio between these two indicators for Canada and the provinces

	Canada	New-foundland and Labrador	Prince Edward Island	Nova Scotia	New Brunswick	Quebec	Ontario	Manitoba	Saskatchewan	Alberta	British Columbia
					in constant 2013 dollars						
Minimum wage weighted by number of employees for each province											
1983	7.87	7.57	7.91	8.03	7.88	8.24	7.61	8.66	9.31	8.40	7.11
1984	7.81	7.25	7.58	7.69	7.50	7.92	7.93	8.35	8.93	8.19	6.84
1985	7.70	7.42	7.44	7.85	7.17	7.58	7.96	8.61	8.83	7.95	6.63
1986	7.53	7.21	7.64	7.62	7.05	7.39	7.78	8.25	8.88	7.69	6.44
1987	7.60	7.01	7.38	7.36	7.09	7.63	7.98	8.32	8.47	7.39	6.25
1988	7.67	7.18	7.23	7.11	6.85	7.69	7.97	8.31	8.10	7.63	6.74
1989	7.71	7.03	7.61	7.66	6.95	7.72	7.88	7.93	7.76	8.18	7.22
1990	7.73	6.74	7.35	7.29	7.13	7.80	7.97	7.59	8.06	7.73	7.41
1991	7.69	6.90	7.12	6.97	7.06	7.68	8.21	7.60	7.86	7.31	7.12
1992	8.14	7.02	7.15	7.58	7.30	7.85	8.96	7.57	7.82	7.80	7.58
1993	8.31	6.90	7.02	7.72	7.20	7.96	9.22	7.37	8.07	7.92	7.88
1994	8.56	6.82	7.04	7.63	7.16	8.27	9.73	7.27	7.93	7.80	7.89
1995	8.64	6.72	6.92	7.53	7.05	8.44	9.71	7.25	7.78	7.63	8.41
1996	8.81	6.74	6.99	7.46	7.47	8.86	9.55	7.48	7.66	7.46	8.92
1997	8.78	7.08	7.40	7.72	7.51	9.01	9.38	7.33	7.89	7.32	8.85
1998	8.75	7.15	7.67	7.69	7.47	9.02	9.30	7.24	7.79	7.37	8.96
1999	8.74	7.14	7.58	7.59	7.35	8.98	9.12	7.69	8.20	7.97	8.91
2000	8.58	6.85	7.55	7.47	7.44	8.77	8.86	7.70	7.99	8.05	8.85
2001	8.48	7.09	7.62	7.46	7.40	8.68	8.60	7.73	7.76	7.86	9.24
2002	8.39	7.19	7.68	7.41	7.31	8.58	8.43	7.92	7.90	7.61	9.42
2003	8.27	7.35	7.73	7.42	7.14	8.66	8.20	8.08	8.17	7.28	9.21
2004	8.31	7.21	7.86	7.74	7.27	8.62	8.38	8.22	7.99	7.18	9.04
2005	8.38	7.20	7.98	7.69	7.22	8.60	8.54	8.29	7.98	7.47	8.86
2006	8.55	7.65	8.10	8.10	7.43	8.62	8.73	8.50	8.60	8.03	8.71
2007	8.63	8.08	8.35	8.38	7.71	8.73	8.86	8.76	8.83	8.02	8.56
2008	8.98	8.68	8.42	8.67	8.29	9.00	9.30	9.08	9.20	8.80	8.38
2009	9.51	9.62	8.91	9.27	8.67	9.48	10.07	9.41	9.70	9.23	8.38
2010	9.86	10.46	9.27	9.81	9.13	9.89	10.62	9.76	9.80	9.24	8.27
2011	9.88	10.38	9.63	10.05	9.61	9.88	10.50	10.00	9.62	9.23	8.71
2012	10.07	10.17	10.10	10.23	9.96	9.89	10.35	10.29	9.68	9.65	9.99
2013	10.14	10.00	10.00	10.26	10.00	10.07	10.25	10.30	10.00	9.82	10.25
Average hourly earnings											
1983	20.45	16.81	14.37	18.05	17.73	19.51	20.28	19.45	21.06	22.69	23.16
1984	20.17	17.13	14.28	17.98	17.77	19.14	20.14	19.72	20.82	22.19	22.55
1985	19.98	17.05	14.07	17.76	17.45	18.89	20.14	19.22	20.33	21.66	22.33
1986	19.67	16.94	13.83	18.00	17.47	18.32	20.00	18.85	20.14	20.85	21.48
1987	19.36	16.22	13.70	17.83	16.98	18.32	19.90	18.30	19.07	20.00	21.12
1988	19.28	16.36	13.96	17.65	16.71	18.44	19.77	18.21	18.56	19.98	20.62
1989	19.35	16.48	14.14	17.37	16.90	18.46	19.90	18.28	18.10	20.14	20.86
1990	19.29	16.08	14.26	17.43	16.68	18.58	19.88	17.98	18.29	20.04	20.35
1991	19.29	16.20	13.82	17.24	16.57	18.21	20.11	17.97	18.02	20.05	20.40
1992	19.68	16.38	14.05	17.72	17.09	18.74	20.54	18.21	18.11	20.47	20.45
1993	19.57	16.78	14.27	17.65	17.14	18.73	20.40	18.14	17.78	20.58	20.05
1994	19.80	17.09	14.29	17.11	16.76	19.16	20.80	17.85	17.87	20.12	20.27
1995	19.67	17.39	15.49	16.79	16.73	18.95	20.65	17.59	17.85	19.42	20.69
1996	19.88	17.90	16.47	16.85	17.08	19.10	20.92	17.46	17.84	19.66	20.72
1997	19.68	17.27	15.54	16.96	17.02	19.07	20.40	17.26	18.50	20.04	20.71
1998	19.83	17.78	16.03	17.83	17.34	18.60	20.87	17.69	18.75	20.86	20.24
1999	19.76	18.42	16.47	18.48	17.49	18.18	20.95	17.95	18.88	21.74	19.21

The ups and downs of minimum wage

Table A.1 (continued)
Real minimum wage, average hourly earnings and ratio between these two indicators for Canada and the provinces

	Canada	New-foundland and Labrador	Prince Edward Island	Nova Scotia	New Brunswick	Quebec	Ontario	Manitoba	Saskatchewan	Alberta	British Columbia
					in constant 2013 dollars						
Average hourly earnings											
2000	19.66	18.05	16.05	18.31	17.49	18.20	20.78	17.75	18.69	21.26	19.41
2001	19.96	19.18	17.15	18.93	18.12	18.89	20.80	17.85	19.11	21.85	19.37
2002	19.90	19.27	17.32	18.82	18.07	18.91	20.69	18.25	18.77	21.45	19.45
2003	19.94	20.17	17.25	18.70	18.10	18.81	20.76	18.38	19.12	21.61	19.42
2004	20.17	20.42	17.67	18.87	17.98	19.06	21.01	18.85	19.29	21.87	19.53
2005	20.44	20.67	17.96	19.19	18.40	19.28	21.09	19.23	19.97	22.57	19.85
2006	20.49	20.79	17.66	18.86	18.46	19.13	21.10	19.20	20.34	22.80	20.02
2007	20.85	21.09	17.94	18.91	18.94	19.71	21.41	19.55	20.84	22.99	20.26
2008	21.14	21.01	17.69	18.92	19.37	20.02	21.52	19.84	21.16	23.69	20.68
2009	21.53	21.16	18.96	18.87	19.76	21.14	21.51	20.29	21.84	24.00	21.29
2010	21.61	21.09	18.81	19.74	19.72	21.08	21.64	20.46	22.22	24.37	21.18
2011	21.74	21.76	19.04	19.76	19.69	21.20	21.75	20.85	22.47	24.53	21.14
2012	21.87	22.18	18.88	19.93	19.73	21.20	21.73	20.98	23.06	24.71	21.59
2013	22.27	22.89	18.82	20.01	19.84	21.58	22.00	20.59	23.71	25.32	22.21
					percentage						
Ratio of the minimum wage to the average hourly earnings											
1983	38.5	45.0	55.0	44.5	44.4	42.2	37.5	44.5	44.2	37.0	30.7
1984	38.7	42.3	53.1	42.8	42.2	41.4	39.4	42.4	42.9	36.9	30.3
1985	38.5	43.5	52.9	44.2	41.1	40.1	39.5	44.8	43.4	36.7	29.7
1986	38.3	42.6	55.3	42.3	40.3	39.8	38.9	43.8	44.1	36.9	30.0
1987	39.3	43.2	53.8	41.3	41.7	41.6	40.1	45.5	44.4	36.9	29.6
1988	39.8	43.9	51.8	40.3	41.0	41.7	40.3	45.6	43.7	38.2	32.7
1989	39.9	42.6	53.9	44.1	41.1	41.8	39.6	43.4	42.9	40.6	34.6
1990	40.0	41.9	51.5	41.8	42.7	42.0	40.1	42.2	44.1	38.6	36.4
1991	39.9	42.6	51.5	40.4	42.6	42.2	40.8	42.3	43.6	36.4	34.9
1992	41.4	42.8	50.9	42.8	42.7	41.9	43.6	41.6	43.2	38.1	37.1
1993	42.4	41.1	49.2	43.7	42.0	42.5	45.2	40.7	45.4	38.5	39.3
1994	43.2	39.9	49.2	44.6	42.7	43.2	46.8	40.7	44.4	38.8	38.9
1995	43.9	38.7	44.7	44.8	42.2	44.6	47.0	41.2	43.6	39.3	40.6
1996	44.3	37.6	42.4	44.3	43.7	46.4	45.7	42.8	43.0	37.9	43.0
1997	44.6	41.0	47.6	45.5	44.1	47.3	46.0	42.5	42.7	36.5	42.7
1998	44.1	40.2	47.9	43.1	43.1	48.5	44.6	40.9	41.5	35.3	44.3
1999	44.3	38.7	46.0	41.1	42.0	49.4	43.5	42.8	43.4	36.7	46.4
2000	43.6	37.9	47.1	40.8	42.5	48.2	42.6	43.3	42.8	37.9	45.6
2001	42.5	37.0	44.4	39.4	40.8	46.0	41.3	43.3	40.6	36.0	47.7
2002	42.2	37.3	44.3	39.4	40.4	45.4	40.7	43.4	42.1	35.5	48.4
2003	41.5	36.4	44.8	39.7	39.4	46.0	39.5	44.0	42.7	33.7	47.4
2004	41.2	35.3	44.5	41.0	40.4	45.2	39.9	43.6	41.4	32.8	46.3
2005	41.0	34.8	44.4	40.1	39.2	44.6	40.5	43.1	39.9	33.1	44.6
2006	41.7	36.8	45.9	42.9	40.3	45.1	41.4	44.3	42.3	35.2	43.5
2007	41.4	38.3	46.6	44.3	40.7	44.3	41.4	44.8	42.4	34.9	42.3
2008	42.5	41.3	47.6	45.8	42.8	45.0	43.2	45.8	43.5	37.1	40.6
2009	44.2	45.5	47.0	49.1	43.9	44.8	46.8	46.4	44.4	38.5	39.4
2010	45.6	49.6	49.3	49.7	46.3	46.9	49.1	47.7	44.1	37.9	39.1
2011	45.4	47.7	50.6	50.9	48.8	46.6	48.3	48.0	42.8	37.6	41.2
2012	46.0	45.9	53.5	51.3	50.5	46.6	47.6	49.0	42.0	39.1	46.3
2013	45.5	43.7	53.1	51.3	50.4	46.7	46.6	50.0	42.2	38.8	46.1

Sources: Statistics Canada, Survey of Employment, Payrolls and Hours (SEPH); Labour Force Survey (LFS); Employment and Social Development Canada (minimum hourly rates by year and by province).

Economic Insights, no. 040, October 2014 • Statistics Canada, Catalogue no. 11-626-X

The Cumulative Earnings of Postsecondary Graduates Over 20 Years: Results by Field of Study

The Cumulative Earnings of Postsecondary Graduates Over 20 Years: Results by Field of Study

by Yuri Ostrovsky and Marc Frenette, Social Analysis and Modelling Division (SAMD)

This article in the *Economic Insights* series reports on the cumulative earnings over a 20-year period of college and bachelor's degree graduates from different fields of study. This article is part of a program at Statistics Canada that examines various dimensions of labour market outcomes of postsecondary graduates.

Introduction

When students graduate from high school, they make at least two educational decisions that affect the rest of their lives. The first is whether to pursue a higher level of education. The literature clearly demonstrates that postsecondary graduates tend to fare better in terms of labour force participation, unemployment, and earnings than do people with less education.

Students who choose to enter a postsecondary program must make a second decision: what to study. Canadian evidence on labour market outcomes by field of study is limited. Research has generally been based on cross-sectional information[1] or on longitudinal data with limited scope;[2] until recently, national-level data have not been available to observe and quantify long-term cumulative outcomes associated with education. However, with the development of new, national longitudinal administrative data, this is now possible. A recent study, in fact, found considerable differences in cumulative earnings across levels of educational attainment.[3]

This study extends that research by examining the cumulative employment earnings of graduates of different fields of study over a 20-year period. Employment earnings include paid wages and salaries, as well as net proceeds from self-employment. The analysis is based on a sample of 15,166 college and bachelor's degree graduates who were aged 26 to 35 in 1991. Information about their level of education and field of study was obtained from their responses to the 1991 Census long questionnaire; information about their employment earnings over the subsequent 20 years was taken from their T1 Income Tax Returns.[4] This study documents three aspects of earnings by field of study: (i) differences in median cumulative earnings across fields of study; (ii) the distribution of cumulative earnings within fields of study; and (iii) the trajectories of annual median earnings within fields of study over the life course of graduates.

Cumulative earnings vary by level and field of study

Bachelor's degree and college graduates earned considerably more than did high school graduates. From 1991 to 2010, the median cumulative earnings (expressed in 2010 constant dollars) of male high school graduates amounted to $882,300 (Table 1). In comparison, male college graduates earned about 1.3 times more ($1,137,000), and male bachelor's degree graduates earned about 1.7 times more ($1,517,200).

Although women generally earned less than men did, the patterns were similar. Women with a bachelor's degree earned $972,500 (about 2.1 times more than high school graduates), and those with a college certificate earned $643,200 (about 1.4 times more than high school graduates).

Postsecondary graduates' earnings also varied considerably across fields of study. For example, men with a bachelor's degree in Engineering earned $1,845,000 over the period, more than twice as much as Fine and Applied Arts graduates, who earned $843,900. Men with a bachelor's degree in Business Administration, Health, and Mathematics and Physical Sciences were also top earners; those who graduated with a degree in Humanities ranked relatively low (second behind Fine and Applied Arts graduates).

The findings were generally similar for women with a bachelor's degree. Top earners again included those who graduated from Business Administration, Mathematics and Physical Sciences, Health, and Engineering. A notable difference between men and women was the relative ranking of Education graduates. Among men, they ranked seventh out of the nine fields. Among women, they ranked fourth—just behind Health graduates and slightly ahead of Engineering graduates. As was the case with male bachelor's degree graduates, the lowest earners among women with a bachelor's degree were those who had studied Fine and Applied Arts.

---

1. See Finnie and Frenette (2003).
2. See Heisz (2003).
3. See Frenette (2014).
4. Although it is possible that some individuals upgraded their education after 1991, they cannot be identified in the tax data. Nevertheless, supplementary analysis of Labour Force Survey data suggests that the prevalence of educational upgrading among this age group is likely quite low. See "Data sources" for a more detailed discussion.

Table 1
Median cumulative earnings by sex, level of education, and field of study

	Men			Women		
	Bachelor's degree	College certificate	High school diploma	Bachelor's degree	College certificate	High school diploma
	2010 constant dollars					
Education	1,290,400	996,600	...	1,044,600	513,500	...
Fine and Applied Arts	843,900	807,200	...	652,100	437,300	...
Humanities	1,144,600	827,500	...	808,200	555,900	...
Social Sciences	1,358,900	1,241,500	...	824,300	563,800	...
Business Administration	1,619,400	1,099,500	...	1,169,100	625,100	...
Life Sciences	1,334,700	753,500	...	844,900	502,300	...
Engineering	1,845,000	1,244,200	...	972,600	718,800	...
Health	1,627,600	1,089,700	...	1,094,000	812,800	...
Mathematics and Physical Sciences	1,607,500	1,128,000	...	1,148,700	793,800	...
All fields of study	1,517,200	1,137,000	882,300	972,500	643,200	458,900

... not applicable

Sources: Statistics Canada, 1991 Census–Longitudinal Worker File and CANSIM table 326-0021.

Male and female college graduates of Fine and Applied Arts programs also ranked near the bottom based on median cumulative earnings (second lowest among men; lowest among women).

For men and women with a college certificate, top earners included graduates of Engineering, Health, Mathematics and Physical Sciences, and Business Administration (as was the case for bachelor's degree graduates). Interestingly, male college Social Sciences graduates ranked second in median cumulative earnings (just behind Engineering graduates). In contrast, the median cumulative earnings of men with a bachelor's degree in Social Sciences were well below the median for all fields of study.

Cumulative earnings also vary substantially within each field

Even if students select the same field of study, their long-term earnings can be quite different. This may be the result of factors such as hours of work, occupation, industry, access to employment networks, abilities and random luck—information not available in the administrative data used in this analysis. Nonetheless, quantifying variability within fields provides perspective on long-term earnings prospects.

To do this, men and women with a college certificate or a bachelor's degree in each field were ranked from lowest to highest in terms of their cumulative earnings. Their "normalized" cumulative earnings are shown in Tables 2 and 3 at the 10th percentile (P10), 25th percentile (P25), median or 50th percentile (P50), 75th percentile (P75), and 90th percentile (P90). Normalized values are expressed relative to the median for all fields combined. The ratios of cumulative earnings of individuals at the 75th and 25th percentiles (the P75/P25 ratio) and at the 90th and 10th percentiles (the P90/P10 ratio) were used as measures of earnings variation within disciplines.

There was considerable earnings variation in cumulative earnings in every discipline, as evidenced by the P75/P25 and the P90/P10 ratios. The P75/P25 ratio ranged from about 1.6 (registered by men with a bachelor's degree in Education) to about 3.8 (men with a bachelor's degree in Fine and Applied Arts). The P90/P10 ratio ranged from about 2.7 (men with a bachelor's degree in Education) to about 16.2 (women with a bachelor's degree in Fine and Applied Arts).

In general, the variation in cumulative earnings within fields of study was higher among women. This was largely attributable to lower earnings at the bottom of the distribution, both in an absolute and a relative sense.

An alternative way to visualize the variability in cumulative earnings within and across fields of study is through a three-dimensional chart. For instance, Figure 1 pertains to men with a bachelor's degree. The fields are sorted from left to right in descending order of cumulative earnings at the 90th percentile.

The "very high" earners (those whose cumulative earnings amounted to at least $2,500,000 over the 20-year period—an annual average of at least $125,000) are at the top (90th percentile) of the distributions in five fields: Business Administration, Mathematics and Physical Sciences, Engineering, Social Sciences, and Health. The cumulative earnings of men at the 90th percentile of the distribution of Business Administration graduates amounted to slightly more than $4,000,000 over the period. This means that about 10% of male graduates with a bachelor's degree in Business and Administration had average annual earnings of $200,000 or more during the two decades.

Some graduates in other fields who were above the 90th percentile in their respective discipline may also have been "very high" earners (cumulative earnings of more than $2,500,000). However, the earnings of graduates of these disciplines (even those at the 90th percentile) were comparatively low. For example, the cumulative

Economic Insights, no. 040, October 2014 • Statistics Canada, Catalogue no. 11-626-X

The Cumulative Earnings of Postsecondary Graduates Over 20 Years: Results by Field of Study

Table 2
Normalized cumulative earnings at selected percentiles (P) by sex and field of study, bachelor's degree graduates

	P10	P25	P50	P75	P90	P75/P25	P90/P10
	normalized value[1]					ratio	
Men							
Education	0.41	0.63	0.85	1.00	1.12	1.58	2.75
Fine and Applied Arts	0.15	0.24	0.56	0.89	1.09	3.77	7.54
Humanities	0.21	0.40	0.75	1.06	1.53	2.62	7.46
Social Sciences	0.41	0.65	0.90	1.21	2.15	1.86	5.21
Business Administration	0.53	0.77	1.07	1.63	2.68	2.10	5.07
Life Sciences	0.46	0.62	0.88	1.10	1.43	1.77	3.14
Engineering	0.64	0.93	1.22	1.57	2.20	1.68	3.44
Health	0.67	0.86	1.07	1.40	1.96	1.63	2.93
Mathematics and Physical Sciences	0.52	0.80	1.06	1.46	2.61	1.82	5.02
All fields of study	0.45	0.71	1.00	1.37	2.19	1.94	4.89
Women							
Education	0.33	0.66	1.07	1.35	1.58	2.06	4.75
Fine and Applied Arts	0.08	0.30	0.67	1.05	1.33	3.51	16.17
Humanities	0.18	0.47	0.83	1.31	1.62	2.76	9.20
Social Sciences	0.25	0.49	0.85	1.24	1.59	2.54	6.32
Business Administration	0.36	0.77	1.20	1.69	2.29	2.21	6.28
Life Sciences	0.12	0.47	0.87	1.22	1.49	2.61	12.60
Engineering	0.30	0.56	1.00	1.58	1.81	2.81	6.13
Health	0.46	0.80	1.13	1.36	1.67	1.71	3.65
Mathematics and Physical Sciences	0.29	0.70	1.18	1.53	2.01	2.19	6.85
All fields of study	0.29	0.58	1.00	1.36	1.69	2.34	5.87

1. Normalized cumulative earnings refer to the cumulative earnings (in 2010 constant dollars) at a given percentile and in a given field of study expressed relative to the median cumulative earnings across all fields of study.
Sources: Statistics Canada, 1991 Census–Longitudinal Worker File and CANSIM table 326-0021.

Table 3
Normalized cumulative earnings at selected percentiles (P) by sex and field of study, college graduates

	P10	P25	P50	P75	P90	P75/P25	P90/P10
	normalized value[1]					ratio	
Men							
Education	0.41	0.62	0.88	1.09	1.49	1.75	3.67
Fine and Applied Arts	0.28	0.47	0.71	1.11	1.44	2.36	5.16
Humanities	0.24	0.43	0.73	0.99	1.28	2.30	5.44
Social Sciences	0.49	0.81	1.09	1.42	1.59	1.76	3.25
Business Administration	0.39	0.67	0.97	1.35	1.81	2.01	4.69
Life Sciences	0.25	0.44	0.66	0.87	1.11	1.99	4.41
Engineering	0.44	0.76	1.09	1.43	1.80	1.89	4.09
Health	0.34	0.72	0.96	1.20	1.45	1.68	4.26
Mathematics and Physical Sciences	0.35	0.64	0.99	1.37	2.13	2.15	6.09
All fields of study	0.38	0.68	1.00	1.36	1.71	2.00	4.46
Women							
Education	0.14	0.43	0.80	1.26	1.66	2.94	11.68
Fine and Applied Arts	0.10	0.31	0.68	1.11	1.51	3.54	14.97
Humanities	0.15	0.45	0.86	1.30	1.88	2.92	12.56
Social Sciences	0.17	0.46	0.88	1.37	1.79	2.97	10.70
Business Administration	0.20	0.52	0.97	1.37	1.80	2.63	9.13
Life Sciences	0.12	0.42	0.78	1.16	1.52	2.80	12.81
Engineering	0.27	0.53	1.12	1.69	2.42	3.17	8.98
Health	0.35	0.79	1.26	1.73	2.11	2.19	6.04
Mathematics and Physical Sciences	0.34	0.74	1.23	1.68	2.46	2.25	7.19
All fields of study	0.21	0.53	1.00	1.46	1.93	2.77	9.43

1. Normalized cumulative earnings refer to the cumulative earnings (in 2010 constant dollars) at a given percentile and in a given field of study expressed relative to the median cumulative earnings across all fields of study.
Sources: Statistics Canada, 1991 Census–Longitudinal Worker File and CANSIM table 326-0021.

Economic Insights, no. 040, October 2014 • Statistics Canada, Catalogue no. 11-626-X
The Cumulative Earnings of Postsecondary Graduates Over 20 Years:
Results by Field of Study

Figure 1
Cumulative earnings of male bachelor's degree graduates by field of study and percentile, 1991 to 2010

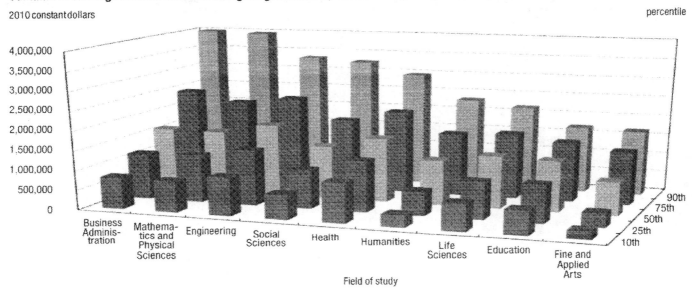

Sources: Statistics Canada, 1991 Census-Longitudinal Worker File and CANSIM table 326-0021.

Figure 2
Cumulative earnings of female bachelor's degree graduates by field of study and percentile, 1991 to 2010

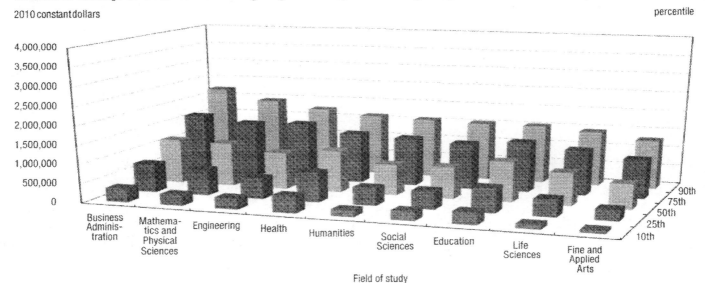

Sources: Statistics Canada, 1991 Census-Longitudinal Worker File and CANSIM table 326-0021.

earnings of men with a bachelor's degree in Education and Fine and Applied Arts who were at the 90th percentile amounted to about $1,700,000 over the 20-year period.

At the opposite end of the spectrum, men at the 10th percentile of the earnings distribution of Fine and Applied Arts graduates earned $222,300 (an annual average of $11,015). Men at the 10th percentile of Humanities graduates earned $311,700 ($15,585 per year).[5]

---

5. These low earnings are not attributable to people leaving Canada for significant periods, because to be included in this analysis, individuals must have appeared in the tax files in at least 18 of the 20 years. Also, earnings include net proceeds from self-employment. Furthermore, these results were not driven by negative net self-employment income among graduates in these disciplines. When earnings were restricted to T4 wages and salaries, men at the 10th percentile of the distribution of Fine and Applied Arts graduates earned even less ($63,300 over the period, or an annual average of $3,165). Finally, since they are men, and since women are generally the primary childcare providers within families, it is unlikely that the results are driven by voluntary withdrawal from the paid labour force to take care of children. One possible explanation that cannot be ruled out is that these graduates simply have not been very successful in the labour market (e.g. they may have relied on social assistance for a substantial portion of the period). Unfortunately, the Longitudinal Worker File does not contain family-level information, which would be required to accurately measure reliance on social assistance.

Table 4
Median annual earnings by sex, field of study, 1991 and 2010

	Bachelor's degree graduates			College graduates		
	1991	2010	Change	1991	2010	Change
	2010 constant dollars					
Men						
Education	51,100	78,100	27,000	39,600	55,200	15,600
Fine and Applied Arts	22,900	42,000	19,100	34,800	42,500	7,700
Humanities	40,800	71,300	30,500	35,700	45,400	9,700
Social Sciences	52,300	78,200	25,900	56,600	72,400	15,800
Business Administration	57,800	95,200	37,400	45,100	60,900	15,800
Life Sciences	51,800	77,800	26,000	29,900	44,800	14,900
Engineering	66,400	105,300	38,900	51,100	70,300	19,200
Health	67,400	92,400	25,000	50,400	61,500	11,100
Mathematics and Physical Sciences	61,900	90,000	28,100	50,900	65,000	14,100
All fields of study	57,400	87,800	30,400	47,600	63,900	16,300
Women						
Education	39,200	69,600	30,400	22,500	31,800	9,300
Fine and Applied Arts	21,300	34,200	12,900	13,400	26,600	13,200
Humanities	31,500	51,800	20,300	23,200	35,600	12,400
Social Sciences	32,600	54,300	21,700	20,700	35,500	14,800
Business Administration	45,500	73,200	27,700	25,700	39,100	13,400
Life Sciences	33,700	58,900	25,200	21,200	29,500	8,300
Engineering	53,900	56,400	2,500	29,800	43,900	14,100
Health	46,800	70,500	23,700	32,700	50,600	17,900
Mathematics and Physical Sciences	46,900	67,100	20,200	36,000	46,800	10,800
All fields of study	38,500	64,100	25,600	26,400	39,600	13,200

Sources: Statistics Canada, 1991 Census–Longitudinal Worker File and CANSIM table 326-0021.

Similar findings are evident for women with a bachelor's degree (Figure 2). Although the ordering of disciplines at the 90th percentile is slightly different, the highest earners were once again from Business and Administration, Mathematics and Physical Sciences, Engineering, and Health. The lowest earners at the 10th percentile were from Fine and Applied Arts and Life Sciences graduates.

Absolute change in median annual earnings similar in most fields

Graduates of the various disciplines likely bring unique skills to the labour market, which may be valued or rewarded differently over time. For example, technical skills may yield greater returns early in one's working life when an individual is at the forefront of the most recent technology; interpersonal skills may yield greater returns at later stages when individuals move into supervisory or managerial positions. Although such factors could have implications for the earnings trajectories of graduates of different fields of study, this is not the case when median annual earnings are tracked through the study period.

Real median annual earnings at the beginning (1991) and end (2010) of the study period are shown in Table 4. Also shown is the change between these two years.

Within each sex and education category, most fields experienced similar absolute changes in median annual earnings over the period. Among men with a bachelor's degree, the absolute change in median annual earnings ranged from $25,000 to $31,000 in six out of the nine fields of study. Similarly, among women with a bachelor's degree, the absolute change in median annual earnings ranged from $20,000 to $28,000 in six out of the nine fields of study. Among college graduates, the absolute changes in median annual earnings were even more consistent across disciplines. Note that the relative changes in median annual earnings (not shown in the table) tended to vary more across fields given the large variation in median annual earnings at the beginning of the period.

Conclusion

A number of key findings emerge from this analysis of the 20-year cumulative earnings of postsecondary graduates by field of study. The first is the considerable variability in median cumulative earnings by level and field of study. Second, even within each field, graduates' earnings varied substantially. Third, the change in median annual earnings was similar for graduates of most fields over the 20-year period.

References

Finnie, R. and M. Frenette. 2003. "Earnings Differences by Major Field of Study: Evidence from Three Cohorts of Recent Canadian Graduates." *Economics of Education Review* 22 (2): 179–192.

Frenette, M. 2014. *An Investment of a Lifetime? The Long-term Labour Market Premiums Associated with a Post-secondary Education.* Analytical Studies Branch Research Paper Series, no. 359. Statistics Canada Catalogue no. 11F0019M. Ottawa: Statistics Canada.

Heisz, A. 2003. *Cohort Effects in Annual Earnings by Field of Study Among British Columbia University Graduates.* Analytical Studies Branch Research Paper Series, no. 200. Statistics Canada Catalogue no. 11F0019M. Ottawa: Statistics Canada.

Economic Insights, no. 040, October 2014 • Statistics Canada, Catalogue no. 11-626-X

The Cumulative Earnings of Postsecondary Graduates Over 20 Years: Results by Field of Study

Data sources, methods and definitions

Data sources

Data from the 1991 Census of Population file, which was linked to the Longitudinal Worker file (LWF), were used in this study. The LWF combines several administrative files, including the T1 Personal files, and is a 10% random sample of the population receiving a T4 Information Slip or filing a T1 Income Tax Return. Individuals who were at least 25 years old on the 1991 Census were linked probabilistically to the LWF with a success rate of more than 75%; however, only 75% of the original sample was maintained in the linked file (based on random selection). The individuals who were successfully linked and maintained in the file were very similar to those in the broader sample of 1991 Census respondents based on several socio-economic characteristics, including highest level of educational attainment.

This study examined 15,166 men and women who, according to the 1991 Census, held a college certificate or a bachelor's degree, were aged 26 to 35 at that time, were born in Canada or came to Canada before age 18, had not attended school in the previous nine months, and appeared in the T1 files in 18 of the next 20 years. The study population consisted of 2,796 men and 3,140 women with a bachelor's degree, and 3,634 men and 5,596 women with a college certificate. The T4 wages and salaries of individuals were tracked in the LWF from 1991 to 2010. Individuals who do not appear in the LWF in a given year were assigned zero T4 wages and salaries.

Although it is possible that some members of the study sample obtained higher educational credentials after 1991, the number is likely small. According to March and September data from the Labour Force Survey (LFS), of all Canadian-born individuals aged 26 to 35 who had a postsecondary credential in 2006 or 2007, 37.6% of them had a bachelor's degree, and 11.3% had a credential above a bachelor's degree. Six years later (in 2012 or 2013), the percentage of individuals who were six years older (but otherwise similar) and had a bachelor's degree was 34.1%, and the percentage with a credential above a bachelor's degree was 15%. The percentage with a college certificate remained steady over the period.

Thus, according to the LFS, about 9% of 26- to 35-year-olds had upgraded their education. However, the current study is restricted to individuals who had not attended school in the nine months before the 1991 Census. In the LFS, 11% of 26- to 35-year-olds who held a bachelor's degree in 2006 and 2007 were still attending school. It is possible that many of them were the people who eventually obtained higher educational credentials, although this cannot be determined because the LFS data are not longitudinal.

Methods

Medians and percentiles are the only statistical techniques employed in this analysis. No regression adjustments were necessary, because the individuals who were compared across and within fields of study shared many important characteristics: they had the same sex; they were about the same age; were born in Canada (or immigrated before age 18); and had the same highest level of education in 1991.

Definitions

Cumulative earnings: This refers to the sum of T4 wages and salaries plus net self-employment income earned from 1991 to 2010, expressed in 2010 constant dollars based on the annual Consumer Price Index (CPI) 2011 basket (CANSIM table 326-0021).

Bachelor's degree: A university degree at the undergraduate level. It excludes university certificates above or below a bachelor's degree, as well as first professional degrees (medicine, dentistry, veterinary medicine, or optometry). This study also excludes graduates of law programs, because a Bachelor of Laws (L.L.B.) is generally considered to be a first professional degree. Non-L.L.B. programs such as legal studies were also excluded, because the specific programs could not be distinguished.

College certificate: A certificate awarded by either a college, CEGEP, or other postsecondary non-university institution (excluding registered apprenticeships or trades certificates). To be consistent with the bachelor's degree category, law programs were excluded.

Field of study: The field of study was identified by the major field of study code used in the 1991 Census. The fields are categorized into nine major groups:

- **Education:** Includes Educational, Recreational and Counselling Services.
- **Fine and Applied Arts:** Includes Fine and Applied Arts.
- **Humanities:** Includes Humanities and Related, as well as No Specialization.
- **Social Sciences:** Includes Social Sciences and Related.
- **Business Administration:** Includes Commerce, Management and Business Administration.
- **Life Sciences:** Includes Agricultural, Biological, Nutritional and Food Sciences.
- **Engineering:** Includes Engineering and Applied Sciences and Science Technologies and Trades
- **Health:** Includes Health Professions and Related.
- **Mathematics and Physical Sciences:** Includes Mathematics, Computer and Physical Sciences.

Unemployment Dynamics Among Canada's Youth

By André Bernard

This *Economic Insights* article reports on the differences between youth and adults in terms of unemployment inflow and outflow rates, factors that contribute to a better understanding of the gap between the unemployment rates of youth and adults. Data from the Labour Force Survey from 1977 to 2012 are used for this analysis.

The youth unemployment rate has historically been higher than that for adults. Recent years, marked by the 2008-2009 recession and the subsequent recovery, have been no exception. In 2012, the unemployment rate of youths aged 15 to 24 was 14.3%, compared with a rate of 6.0% for workers aged 25 to 54 and workers aged 55 or older (Chart 1).

The gap between the unemployment rates of youths and adults has not decreased since the early 1990s, and has even increased slightly since 2010 (Chart 2). In 2012, the youth unemployment rate was 2.4 times that of workers aged 25 to 54, the biggest gap recorded since 1977.[1] The widening of the gap between the two unemployment rates is due primarily to the fact that the level of employment among young people had still not, by 2012, returned to its pre-recession level (Bloskie and Gellatly 2012). It is worth noting that the labour force participation rate of youth is historically lower than that of adults, mainly because a majority of young people attend school (Chart 3).[2]

The historical difference between youth and adult unemployment rates is not unique to Canada. In 2011, youth in all member countries of the Organisation for Economic Co-operation and Development (OECD) posted higher unemployment rates than did adults. Among G7 countries, Italy, the United Kingdom, and France reported the largest gaps between youth and adults, while Germany and Japan reported the smallest. (Chart 4).[3]

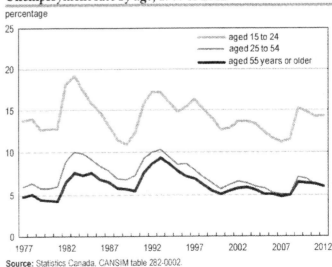

Chart 1
Unemployment rate by age, 1977 to 2012

Source: Statistics Canada, CANSIM table 282-0002.

---

1. In absolute difference, the youth unemployment rate was 8.3 percentage points higher than that of adults in 2012. On average, between 1977 and 2012, the difference between these two unemployment rates was 7.0 percentage points.
2. This gap has also widened since 2008. The labour force participation rate for youth aged 15 to 24 years fell from 67.5% in 2008 to 63.6% in 2012, while it remained stable among workers aged 25 to 54 and increased among workers aged 55 or older. The drop in the labour market participation of youth is due mainly to increased full-time school attendance.
3. The data for Canada and the other countries listed have been adjusted for comparability. For this reason, the Canadian data in this graph may differ slightly from the data normally published by Statistics Canada.

Why is the unemployment rate among youth consistently higher than the unemployment rate among adults? One way to address this question is to examine the differences between youth and adults in terms of unemployment inflow rates, which provide information on the incidence of unemployment, and unemployment outflow rates, which provide information on the duration of unemployment.[4]

Unemployment inflow rates are higher when people who are employed or who are not in the labour force are more likely to become unemployed, for example, when a group of workers is at greater risk of being laid off. Higher inflow rates therefore contribute to increasing the unemployment rate. If unemployment spells that go along with these inflows are short, the employment situation will be one in which a great many individuals periodically go through unemployment but come out of it relatively quickly.

Low unemployment outflow rates also contribute to increasing the unemployment rate and normally reflect difficulties that people seeking a job encounter during their job search. As a result, spells of unemployment tend to increase in duration, and this can have negative consequences in the long term, such as financial problems, skills erosion, and some degree of social exclusion.[5]

This article examines the relative contributions of the unemployment inflow and outflow rates of youth and adults in explaining the differences in the unemployment rates of these two groups. To this end, data from the Labour Force Survey (LFS) from 1977 to 2012 are used.

Inflows to unemployment are higher among youth than adults

A significant proportion of unemployed youth are people entering the labour market for the first time, most often after having completed their education. These young people have never worked and most often experience a period of unemployment of varying duration before finding a first job. This situation is much less common among adult workers.

In 2012, more than one-quarter (28.1%) of unemployed young people between 15 and 24 years of age were youth who had never worked.[6] For workers aged 25 to 54 and workers aged 55 or older, these proportions were 5.4% and 1.7%, respectively. For these young people, unemployment is linked to seeking a first job and is not the result of the economic situation, unless their job search is prolonged.

What is the situation regarding inflows to unemployment of people who are employed? Table 1 shows the proportion of youth and adults who were employed in a given month but unemployed the next month. It also shows the proportion of youth and adults who were employed in a given month but who had left the labour force the next month.

Young workers are generally more likely to become unemployed than are adult workers. In 2012, the average monthly inflow to unemployment of employed youth was 2.6%. This means that, on average, 2.6% of youth who were working in a given month in 2012 became unemployed in the following month.[7]

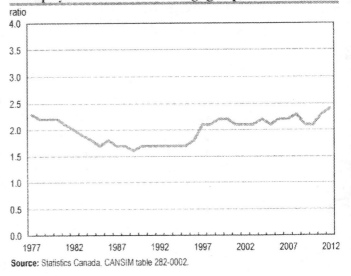

Chart 2
Ratio of unemployment rate of 15-to-24 age group to unemployment rate of 25-to-54 age group, 1977 to 2012

Source: Statistics Canada, CANSIM table 282-0002.

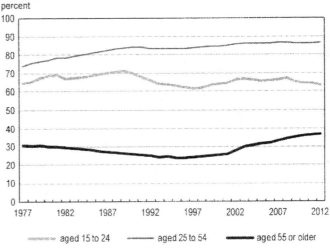

Chart 3
Labour force participation rate by age, 1977 to 2012

Source: Statistics Canada, CANSIM table 282-0002.

---

4. Baker, Corak, and Heisz (1998) and Tille (1998) examined differences in incidence and duration to explain the differences between Canadian and U.S. unemployment rates, while Elsby, Hobijn, and Sahin (2008) used a similar approach to explain variations in the unemployment rates of OECD countries.
5. See, for example, Tille (1998) and Dubé (2004).
6. On average, in the last 15 years, almost one-quarter (22.9%) of unemployed youth were persons who had never worked.
7. The LFS is a rotating panel survey. Households are interviewed for six consecutive months. The data in Tables 1 and 2 and Graphs 5 and 6 are obtained by matching the responses from individuals who are respondents for each pair of consecutive months and examining the transitions related to labour force status from one month to the next. The data in Graphs 7, 8, and 9 are obtained by matching the responses from respondents for periods of four consecutive months. Controls are in place to ensure that the transitions identified relate to the same person. The methodology employed is similar to that used in Chan, Morissette, and Frenette (2011).

In comparison, the inflow to unemployment of workers aged 25 to 54 and workers aged 55 or older was significantly lower. In 2012, on average from one month to the next, 1.1% of workers aged 25 to 54 left or lost their jobs and became unemployed.

While employed youth are more likely to become unemployed, they are also more likely to leave the labour force without going through a spell of unemployment. When they do this, it is in most cases because they are returning to full-time education. In 2012, 4.2% of youth employed in a given month were no longer part of the labour force the following month and were instead attending school full-time. It is likely that these young people who leave the labour force to attend school will rejoin it later on.

In addition, the proportion of youth who were employed and who left the labour force without becoming full-time students was not very different from the proportion observed among workers aged 25 to 54. This result appears at odds with the notion that young people are less inclined to participate in the labour market than adults, if one excludes those youths who do not participate in the labour market because they are attending school full-time.

Chart 4
Unemployment rate, total population and youth aged 15 to 24, G7 countries, 2011

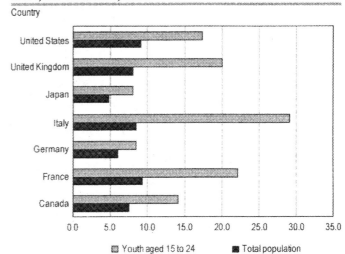

Source: Organisation for Economic Co-operation and Development.

Table 1
Changes in status from one month to the next, employed persons, 2007 to 2012

	1977 to 1989	1990 to 1999	2000 to 2006	2007	2008	2009	2010	2011	2012
				percent					
Aged 15 to 24									
Still employed	91.6	90.9	90.7	91.6	91.7	91.3	91.9	91.9	91.8
Became unemployed	3.0	2.9	2.7	2.4	2.6	2.8	2.5	2.4	2.6
Left the labour force									
Full-time studies	3.6	4.5	4.8	4.3	4.1	4.3	4.3	4.2	4.2
Other reasons	1.8	1.6	1.8	1.6	1.6	1.5	1.4	1.5	1.5
Total	100.0	100.0	100.0	100.0	100.0	100.0	100.0	100.0	100.0
Aged 25 to 54									
Still employed	97.2	97.2	97.1	97.5	97.5	97.2	97.5	97.5	97.6
Became unemployed	1.3	1.4	1.2	1.1	1.0	1.4	1.1	1.0	1.1
Left the labour force									
Full-time studies	F	F	F	F	F	F	F	F	F
Other reasons	1.3	1.2	1.5	1.3	1.3	1.3	1.2	1.2	1.2
Total	100.0	100.0	100.0	100.0	100.0	100.0	100.0	100.0	100.0
Aged 55 or older									
Still employed	96.5	96.0	94.8	95.9	95.8	95.9	96.1	95.9	96.3
Became unemployed	0.8	1.0	0.9	0.8	0.8	1.0	0.9	0.9	0.8
Left the labour force									
Full-time studies	F	F	F	F	F	F	F	F	F
Other reasons	2.6	3.0	4.2	3.3	3.3	3.1	3.0	3.1	2.8
Total	100.0	100.0	100.0	100.0	100.0	100.0	100.0	100.0	100.0

Note: Estimates for the percentage of workers aged 25 to 54 and aged 55 or older who return to full-time education are too small and therefore too unreliable to be published.
Source: Statistics Canada, Labour Force Survey.

Youth are twice as likely as adults to be laid off

The majority of youth (60.4% in 2012) who were employed one month and unemployed the next month made this transition because they were laid off.[8] It is therefore important to examine the trends in the layoff rates among youth and adults.

Young workers are more likely than adult workers to be laid off by their employers. The monthly layoff rate among youth was 3.5% in 2012.[9] This rate is more than twice the rate of 1.3% for workers aged 25 to 54 and the rate of 1.5% for workers aged 55 or older (Chart 5). Since 1977, the annual layoff rate for youth aged 15 to 24 has been between 2.0 to 2.7 times that of workers aged 25 to 54.

Since it is less expensive for an employer to replace a worker who has just been hired than a more experienced worker, the employer may be more inclined, when workforce reductions are occurring, to lay off a worker with less seniority. The link between seniority and the likelihood of being laid off was in fact documented in a recent study.[10] It is therefore possible that part of the difference in layoff rates between young workers and adult workers is due to the lower seniority, on average, of young workers.

To verify this assumption, the layoff rates of youth and adults who were part of a sample of workers with less than one year of seniority with their employers are examined. For this category of newly hired workers, the gap between the layoff rates of youth and adults persists but is considerably smaller. Indeed, the layoff rate was 4.8% for youth in 2012 compared to 3.1% for workers aged 25 to 54 and 5.6% for workers aged 55 or older (Chart 6). Thus, youth are at higher risk of being laid off more because of their lack of seniority with the employer than because of their age.[11]

It is worth noting that, until the late 1990s, there was little or no difference in the layoff rates of youth and adults among workers with less than one year of seniority. A gap appeared beginning in the early 2000s. However, the difference is significantly less than that observed among workers as a whole, regardless of seniority.

Unemployment outflow rates are higher among youth

Table 2 shows the percentage of workers in a given month who found work the following month, and the percentage of workers who left the labour force. These percentages are unemployment outflow rates. Everything else being equal, the lower the outflow rates, the longer the spells of unemployment and the higher the unemployment rates.

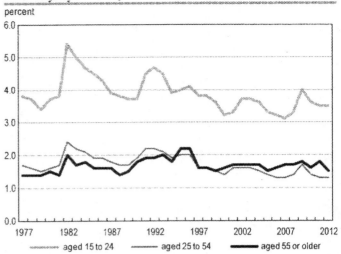

Chart 5
Monthly layoff rates, 1977 to 2012

Source: Statistics Canada, Labour Force Survey.

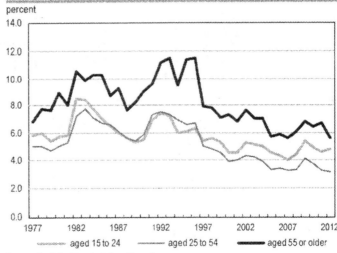

Chart 6
Monthly layoff rates, workers with less than one year of seniority, 1977 to 2012

Source: Statistics Canada, Labour Force Survey.

Unemployment outflow rates for youth are higher than those for adults because young people are more likely than unemployed adults to find work and, especially, because youth are more likely to leave the labour force to attend school full time. These trends have been observed for many years.[12]

---

8. Normally, people who leave a job voluntarily do so either to take on another job or to leave the labour force. Some young people, however, leave their jobs to become unemployed. In a number of cases, youth make this transition in order to devote more time to finding a better-quality job. This transition can prove beneficial in the long term (Topel and Ward 1992).
9. Persons who are laid off are those who were employed in a given month and then were without a job (either unemployed or out of the labour force) the following month, and who reported that a layoff was the cause of their termination of employment.
10. See Chan, Morissette, and Frenette (2011).
11. This hypothesis was also verified using multivariate analysis. The results for a logistic regression model of the probability of being laid off that used age group as the single explanatory variable were compared to the results obtained when the variables of seniority, education, industry, and union membership were added progressively. The results show that approximately two-thirds of the difference in the probabilities of being laid off of youth and adults aged 25 to 54 years, between 2007 and 2012, is due to differences in seniority.
12. Even when individuals who were studying full-time in one or the other of two consecutive months are excluded from the sample, results show that youth are more likely than adults to transition from unemployment to employment.

Economic Insights, no. 024, June 2013 • Statistics Canada, Catalogue no. 11-626-X
Unemployment Dynamics Among Canada's Youth

Table 2
Changes in status from one month to the next, unemployed persons, 2007 to 2012

	1977 to 1989	1990 to 1999	2000 to 2006	2007	2008	2009	2010	2011	2012
				percent					
Aged 15 to 24									
Employed	23.2	21.1	27.1	29.8	27.4	21.9	22.1	22.2	23.2
Still unemployed	57.3	55.4	45.7	44.3	45.4	52.2	50.8	50.8	49.1
Left the labour force									
Full-time studies	8.2	13.1	17.0	15.9	15.9	16.1	16.7	16.9	17.4
Other reasons	11.4	10.3	10.3	9.9	11.3	9.8	10.3	10.1	10.3
Total	100.0	100.0	100.0	100.0	100.0	100.0	100.0	100.0	100.0
Aged 25 to 54									
Employed	19.7	18.2	23.8	24.3	23.6	19.8	19.3	20.3	20.6
Still unemployed	65.7	68.0	60.3	60.0	60.8	66.0	67.1	64.9	64.3
Left the labour force									
Full-time studies	F	F	F	F	F	F	F	F	F
Other reasons	13.9	12.4	14.2	13.8	13.8	12.3	11.9	12.8	13.4
Total	100.0	100.0	100.0	100.0	100.0	100.0	100.0	100.0	100.0
Aged 55 or older									
Employed	14.1	13.2	18.0	17.8	17.8	15.0	15.3	15.0	15.8
Still unemployed	64.8	67.0	58.9	60.2	61.0	66.0	66.9	66.1	65.3
Left the labour force									
Full-time studies	F	F	F	F	F	F	F	F	F
Other reasons	20.7	19.3	22.4	21.2	20.3	18.3	17.4	18.6	18.5
Total	100.0	100.0	100.0	100.0	100.0	100.0	100.0	100.0	100.0

Note: Estimates for the percentage of unemployed individuals aged 25 to 54 and aged 55 or older who return to full-time education are too small and therefore too unreliable to be published.
Source: Statistics Canada, Labour Force Survey.

In 2012, an average of 23.2% of workers aged 15 to 24 who were unemployed one month found work the following month. This is a higher percentage than that observed among workers aged 25 to 54 (20.6%) and workers aged 55 or older (15.8%). Even in 2009, coming out of the recession, the outflow rates from unemployment to employment were higher for youth than for the other two age groups.

Each month, workers, particularly young workers, can terminate their spell of unemployment by leaving the labour force. In 2012, that proportion was 27.7% for youth compared to 15.1% for workers aged 25 to 54 and 19.0% for workers aged 55 or older.

However, most unemployed youth who leave the labour force are full-time students who will likely rejoin the labour market after a period of time. The proportion of unemployed youth leaving the labour force to attend school full-time has increased significantly over the years. While this proportion was, on average, 8.2% between 1977 and 1989, it was 17.4% in 2012. In contrast, there has been little change over time in the proportion of unemployed youth who leave the labour force without becoming full-time students, with that proportion always remaining below the corresponding proportion for unemployed workers aged 25 to 54.

New spells of unemployment are more likely to be short for youth

The unemployment outflow rates presented so far are averages for all unemployed workers, regardless of the initial duration of unemployment. In this section, the outflow rates within three months of new spells of unemployment are examined. A new unemployment spell can be the result of a layoff, a resignation, or a new entry into the labour market. The goal is to evaluate the extent to which new spells of unemployment among youth and adults are likely to be of short duration.

For all age groups, most new unemployment spells last less than three months. However, youth are proportionally more likely than adults to experience relatively short spells of unemployment. In 2012, 79.4% of youth who became unemployed were no longer unemployed less than three months later. In comparison, that proportion was 67.6% for workers aged 25 to 54 and 70.6% for workers aged 55 or older (Chart 7). Every year since 1982, the outflow rates within three months of new spells of unemployment have been higher for youth than for adults.

Youth who become unemployed are more likely than adults to find employment quickly

The end of an unemployment spell can coincide with the start of a new job or with an exit from the labour force, for example, when a young person stops looking for work in order to return to school. Even when excluding unemployment outflows that result in leaving the labour force, outflow rates within three months of new spells of unemployment are higher among youth than adults. In 2012, 67.6% of youth who became unemployed and who did not subsequently leave the labour force found a job in less than three months. For workers aged 25 to 54 and workers aged 55 or older, these percentages were, respectively, 58.0% and 54.9% (Chart 8). Outflow rates within three months of new unemployment spells, excluding transitions out of the labour force, have been higher for youth than for adults every year since 1978.[13]

Shorter spells of unemployment for youth aged 15 to 19 than for workers aged 20 to 24

Higher outflow rates are observed for both youth ages 15 to 19 and workers aged 20 to 24, the latter age group being composed of a greater number who have completed their education.

In 2012, the outflow rates within three months of new unemployment spells, excluding transitions out of the labour force, were 65.5% for youth 15 to 19 years of age and 70.0% for workers 20 to 24 years of age (Chart 9). Both of these rates were higher than the 58.0% rate posted for workers aged 25 to 54. Since the early 1990s, outflow rates within three months of new spells of unemployment for youth aged 15 to 19 and workers aged 20 to 24 have followed similar trends.

Spells of unemployment are more likely to last longer during a recession

For both youth and adults, outflow rates within three months of new spells of unemployment tend to decline during recessions and increase during times of economic growth.[14] The lows during the recession of 2008-2009 for the three age groups were not, however, as low as those observed during previous recessions. On the other hand, the outflow rates posted in 2012 for the three age groups were all still below those recorded prior to the 2008-2009 recession.

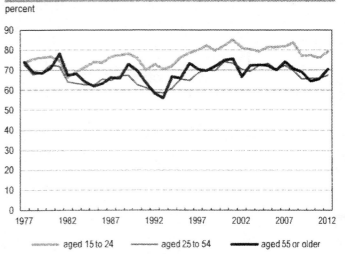

Chart 7
Outflow rates after three months of new spells of unemployment, 1977 to 2012

Source: Statistics Canada, Labour Force Survey.

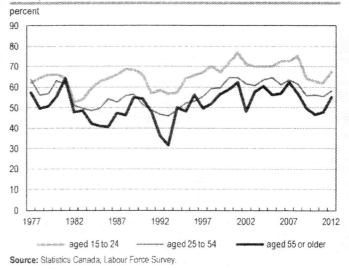

Chart 8
Outflow rates after three months of new spells of unemployment, excluding transitions out of the labour force, 1977 to 2012

Source: Statistics Canada, Labour Force Survey.

---

13. The same observation applies to both men and women. Both young women and young men have outflow rates within three months of new spells of unemployment that are higher than those of their older counterparts.
14. This finding is consistent with that of a recent study showing that outflow rates from unemployment to employment are procyclical in Canada and in the United States (Campolieti 2011).

Generally, outflow rates within three months of new unemployment spells show greater cyclical variability when transitions out of the labour force are excluded. This result is due to the fact that transitions to employment are more closely tied to economic conditions than are transitions out of the labour force.[15]

Conclusion

The findings presented in this article demonstrate that there are marked differences in the incidence and duration of unemployment between youth and adults. Youth spend less time unemployed than adults, in part because they are more inclined to leave the labour force in order to return to full-time education and in part because they are more likely than unemployed adults to find a job within a short time.

The gap in unemployment rates of youth and adults is due more to the higher unemployment inflow rates among youth, a phenomenon linked largely to their higher risk of layoff and their periodic departures from the labour force to attend school full-time. Their higher risk of layoff is explained in large part by their lower seniority with employers.

Having a job does not mean that that job is well paid or well matched to competencies acquired through education.[16] Furthermore, this study does not examine the causes of the variations in unemployment inflow rates and outflow rates. A recent study showed that fluctuations in unemployment were related more to fluctuations in the duration of unemployment than to variations in the incidence of unemployment, especially in the case of youth (Campolieti 2011). A more in-depth analysis of the factors associated with changes in the duration of unemployment would therefore provide additional insight into the dynamics of youth unemployment.

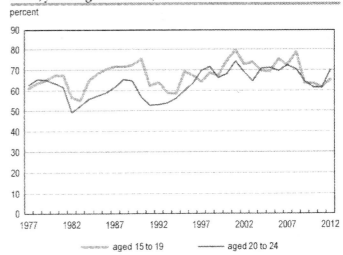

Chart 9
Outflow rates after three months of new spells of unemployment, excluding transitions out of the labour force, youth aged 15 to 24, 1977 to 2012

Source: Statistics Canada, Labour Force Survey.

---

15. It is nevertheless necessary to interpret the significant annual variations observed among adults aged 55 or older with caution given the smaller size of the sample of persons in this age group who remain in the labour force for three consecutive months.
16. A recent study analyzes the various measures of youth under-employment (CGA-Canada 2012), while another presents the trends in youth and adult wages over the last three decades (Morissette, Picot, and Lu 2013).

References

Baker, M., M. Corak, and A. Heisz. 1998. "The Labour Market Dynamics of Unemployment Rates in Canada and the United States." *Canadian Public Policy* 24 (Supplement 1): S72–S89.

Bloskie, C., and G. Gellatly. 2012. *Recent Developments in the Canadian Economy: Fall 2012*. Economic Insights, no. 19. Statistics Canada Catalogue no. 11-626-X. Ottawa: Statistics Canada.

Campolieti, M. 2011. "The ins and outs of unemployment in Canada, 1976-2008." *Canadian Journal of Economics* 44 (4): 1331–1349.

Certified General Accountants Association of Canada (CGA). 2012. *Youth Unemployment in Canada: Challenging Conventional Thinking?* CGA-Canada.

Chan, P.C.W., R. Morissette, and M. Frenette. 2011. *Workers Laid-off During the Last Three Recessions: Who Were They, and How Did They Fare?* Analytical Studies Branch Research Paper Series, no. 337. Statistics Canada Catalogue no. 11F0019M. Ottawa: Statistics Canada.

Dubé, V. 2004. "Sidelined in the labour market." *Perspectives on Labour and Income* 5 (4): 5–11. Statistics Canada Catalogue no. 75-001-X.

Elsby, M., B. Hobijn, and A. Sahin. 2008. *Unemployment Dynamics in the OECD*. NBER Working Paper Series, no. 14617. Cambridge, Massachusetts: National Bureau of Economic Research.

Morissette, R., G. Picot, and Y. Lu. 2013. *The Evolution of Canadian Wages over the Last Three Decades*. Analytical Studies Branch Research Paper Series, no. 347. Statistics Canada Catalogue no. 11F0019M. Ottawa: Statistics Canada.

Topel, R.H., and M.P. Ward. 1992. "Job Mobility and the Careers of Young Men." *The Quaterly Journal of Economics* 107 (2): 439–479.

Tille, C. 1998. "Decomposition of the Unemployment Gap between Canada and the United States: Duration or Incidence?" *Canadian Public Policy* 24 (Supplement 1): S90–S102.

60